A Toolkit for
Action Research

A Toolkit for
Action Research

SANDRA M. ALBER

ROWMAN & LITTLEFIELD PUBLISHERS, INC.
Lanham • Boulder • New York • Toronto • Plymouth, UK

Published by Rowman & Littlefield Publishers, Inc.
A wholly owned subsidary of The Rowman & Littlefield Publishing Group, Inc.
4501 Forbes Boulevard, Suite 200, Lanham, Maryland 20706
http://www.rowmanlittlefield.com

Estover Road, Plymouth PL6 7PY, United Kingdom

British Library Cataloguing in Publication Information Available

Library of Congress Cataloging-in-Publication Data

Alber, Sandra M., 1945-
    A toolkit for action research / Sandra M. Alber.
        p. cm.
    Includes bibliographical references.
    ISBN 978-1-4422-0693-9 (pbk. : alk. paper) — ISBN 978-1-4422-0694-6 (electronic)
    1. Action research in education. 2. Education—Research. 3. Educational reports. I. Title.
    LB1028.4.A43 2011
    370.72—dc22   2010017908

♾ ™ The paper used in this publication meets the minimum requirements of American National
Standard for Information Sciences—Permanence of Paper for Printed Library Materials, ANSI/
NISO Z39.48-1992.

Printed in the United States of America

This work is dedicated to
Emma Elizabeth Loewe and Keenan James Loewe.
Thank you for coming into this world.
Your Grandma Sandy loves you.

Contents

Preface

The purpose of this book is to facilitate the completion of action research studies. The book provides a series of frames that were designed to guide action researchers from the beginning of a project, selecting a topic for study, to completion of the project and editing final reports. The tools in the book are based on the assumption that action research can best be tackled one step at a time. Too often students and in-service professionals believe doing an action research project requires using a quasi-experimental design to do a research project on their own with little support. Both students and practicing professionals in professional development schools are often initially overwhelmed by the thought of doing an action research project. I tell them, as I tell the researchers using this book, that doing action research is like eating a pizza. You take one slice at a time and then take one bite at a time. Eating the whole pizza at one time is quite likely to make one sick. This book is offered as a series of tools to help investigators focus and work on their studies one piece and one portion of that piece at a time.

In practice, this book resulted from working with teachers, administrators, nurses, therapists, and other helping professionals in university and professional development settings. I came to facilitating action research studies from the perspective of a former elementary school teacher who taught children writing as a process. As I began working with helping professionals, I saw their angst about doing action research. They tended to believe that I would give them assignments and lecture on what they should and should not do. Of course, my task was to help guide them through their own studies in a series of meaningful and helpful steps that would ultimately result in the completion of their study. As I worked through the steps over eighteen years of supporting action researchers, I developed frames that the researchers whom I have mentored found meaningful and helpful. I have organized the resulting frames in a sequential order that works well for the researchers whom I have guided through projects.

HOW TO USE THIS BOOK

This book is for use in college classes and professional development settings. In addition, it may be useful to individuals conducting field studies and theses. I have successfully used the frames in this book to guide people engaged in each of the endeavors mentioned in this paragraph. The book was designed to serve as a companion text with more traditional textbooks on action research. One such text is Daniel Tomal's *Action Research in Education.*

The book is organized into five sections, which complement the five sections that I teach in my classes. These five sections are the following: introduction to the research project, literature review, methodology, findings, and discussion. I believe that the frames within each section have a flow common to many project formats. In spite of this belief, I realize that completing all frames in all sections may not fit all project formats. For example, when I work with teachers in professional development schools, their literature review is less formal and less extensive than when I work with graduate students doing their capstone project.

The book is designed to be written in. All the frames are presented with space for the student to actually fill out and use with their action research projects. My hope is that by the end of the course, the book is dog-eared with notes in the margins and the forms completed. In that way, the professor will know that the book has helped his or her students become lifelong classroom researchers.

Acknowledgments

I wish to thank those who have provided feedback on the frames included in this book. First, thank you to the students at Oakland University who used the frames in completing their projects. Second, thank you to the staff and faculty in the professional development schools in Detroit and Dearborn Public Schools with whom I've worked. Third, thank you to Bess Kypros, Sally Edgerton (posthumous), and Don Miller (posthumous), colleagues with whom I discussed mentoring action researchers over the past eighteen years. Thank you to Daniel Tomal for his thoughtful suggestions and e-mail conversations and for his insights when the text was in its final stages.

Thank you for the support of my colleagues in the Department of Human Development and Child Studies at Oakland University for their assistance that resulted in my sabbatical leave. Thank you to Erin L. Howe and Michelle R. Brubaker, my daughters who have completed action research projects as parts of their master's degrees, for their time and valuable insights. I appreciate your input on the frames and how they might have helped or hindered in the completion of your studies.

Maera Stratton, I appreciate your contributions to the early draft of this book. Finally, a huge thank you goes to Patti Belcher, my editor and guide, for helping bring the book to print. Patti, you are a patient and wonderful mentor and editor. To all of you, I appreciate your honesty and thoughtfulness.

SETTING THE STAGE FOR THE ACTION RESEARCH PROJECT

The first steps in an action research project are to focus the study and to set the stage for the study. There are common features to the first phase of most action research studies. These common features include selecting a specific topic, narrowing the topic to be studied, developing a research question, identifying the purpose of the study, writing a thesis statement, identifying the problems surrounding the study, describing the context of the study, and identifying central issues or subtopics surrounding the specific focus of the research project. By completing each of the frames presented in section 1 in the order that they are presented, you will have identified and considered the key components of phase 1 of the study. In the paragraphs that follow you will find brief explanations and rationales for completing each frame in section 1.

Section 1 begins with two frames to help you select your topic for study. Frame 1.1, "Finding My Topic—Part 1," helps you consider topics of interest and importance to you. You will complete the first frame by briefly responding to each of the sixteen prompts. It is important to be honest with yourself as you reply to the prompts. If a prompt fails to provoke thoughts at first, you should skip it and return to it later. Completing the other prompts may induce thoughts about the skipped prompt. If, after considerable thought, no response to the prompt is forthcoming, you will pass over that prompt. Frame 1.1 is not a "test" or an assignment to be completed. Rather, it is a tool to help you consider interesting, worthwhile, and meaningful topics.

Frame 1.2, "Finding My Topic—Part 2," assists you in thinking about the topics recorded in Frame 1.1.

Frame 1.2 is included to help you evaluate the replies made in the first frame. You should reply frankly to the eight questions. After conscientiously thinking about this set of replies, you will complete the sentence stem at the bottom of the page. The frame starts by helping you look broadly at your research area. By answering the questions thoughtfully, you will gradually narrow a broad field of interest into a more manageable topic of study. By carefully evaluating and narrowing the possible topics to a single topic, you will be ready to set the stage for the study. Again, the intent of Frame 1.2 is to help you consider study options, rather than to be an exercise to complete.

Following the second frame you will find Frame 1.3, "Developing a Thesis Statement," which was designed to aid you in writing a thesis statement. The thesis statement will help you and your readers see where the study is going. You will fill in each of the five boxes in the order presented on the page. The "specific focus" identified in the second box is repeated in the third box. You will then combine your specific focus with the contents of the fourth box, assertions about the subject, to develop your thesis statement. The final box will contain your thesis statement.

Completion of Frame 1.4, "Asking Your Research Question," will help you write a research question or questions. In the first box simply record the specific topic. After careful consideration of the prompts in the second and third boxes, you will list or bullet your thoughts about how your specific topic relates to issues in your workplace responsibilities and what you want to know about the specific topic. Taking time to seriously consider the research question(s) and the ideas leading to the question(s) is important because it directs the flow of your project and leads you through a thoughtful investigation of a question of importance to you and your work. In the fourth box you will record the thesis statement. Considering the thesis statement will help you think about a research question. Having thoughtfully completed these first four boxes, you will evaluate the responses in these boxes and write the research question(s). The next box contains a series of questions to evaluate the first draft of your research question. Hopefully, you will be able to answer each question with a "yes." If that is not the case, you will need to revise the research question. Once you are able to answer "yes" to all the questions in the sixth box, you will write the revised research question in the final box of Frame 1.4.

Frame 1.5, "Preparing to Discuss the Problems and Context of Your Study," aids you in considering the problems surrounding the study and describing the context of your study. In each of the boxes provided, you will honestly write a response to the prompt. By considering the challenges, problems, and political, policy, and cultural issues surrounding your problem, along with the local and workplace context, both you and your readers have a deeper understanding of your study.

Frame 1.6, "Describing the Purpose of Your Research," helps you understand the connection between the research question and the purpose of the study. Often, beginning action researchers confuse the purpose of the study with their professional work goals. The goals are important and will help direct your study, but in the initial phase of your action research project it is important to address the purpose of the study rather than the goals. The purpose of doing an action research project is to learn something. In an action research study, the purpose is directly related to the research question(s). Another way of thinking about the purpose of a study is to think that the purpose of your study is to answer your research question. By completing the loops in the order presented, you will make a connection from the research question to the purpose of your study.

You may or may not choose to use Frame 1.7, "Identifying Related Aspects of Your General Topic—Method 1." Frame 1.8 accomplishes the same tasks as Frame 1.7. Both frames facilitate identifying central, related issues in your study. Choose the frame that is most helpful to you. If you elect to complete Frame 1.7, you should consider the specific topic and complete the frame by jotting down key issues that come to mind as you think about the topic. Action researchers often think about theories, research, culture, human development, best practices, and key concepts as they consider what to put in the loops in Frame 1.7. If necessary, you can add additional loops to the diagram. Completing this frame focuses you and your reader on key issues surrounding the specific topic. It also helps you begin to think about elements to be discussed in phase 2 of the study, which is a review of the related literature.

Frame 1.8, "Identifying Related Aspects of Your General Topic—Method 2," is a more linear way to identify central, related issues in your study. Seven labeled boxes are provided for you to list your thoughts on the cultural, development, research, theoretical, and practice issues surrounding your specific topic. Again, this frame is an alternative to Frame 1.7. You will not need to complete both 1.7 and 1.8.

Finally, the last frame in section 1, Frame 1.9, "Organizing for Writing," is a form created to help you prepare to write the first section of the project plan and report. After completing each of the five boxes in Frame 1.9, you will create a schematic web. (Frame 1.7, "Identifying Related Aspects of the General Topic—Method 1," is an example of a schematic web.) The items identified in the five boxes are put into the web, thus creating a visual method of examining the connection between each of the key components of phase 1 of your study. An alternative to a schematic web is a traditional outline; if you choose to construct a traditional outline, make sure to include each of the key elements identified in the five boxes.

Having completed the frames in section 1, you are now ready to write the first draft of section 1 of the action research project.

Finding My Topic—Part 1

DISCREPANCIES

1. Consider any discrepancies you have noticed between your practice or craft knowledge and book knowledge. List a few instances below.

2. Consider any discrepancies you have noticed between your planned outcomes and unexpected outcomes. List a few instances below.

3. Consider any discrepancies you have noticed between your present situation and goals or missions of your workplace. List a few instances below.

4. Consider any discrepancies you have noticed between outcomes and state and/or local standards, mandates, or guidelines. List a few instances below.

PROFESSIONAL GROWTH

  5. List professional strengths that you would like to develop.

  6. List any professional situations that you would like to cope with better.

  7. List professional practices of which you would like to have a deeper understanding.

  8. List some things you would like to improve in your practice.

Frame 1.1 FINDING MY TOPIC—PART 1 (continued)

ISSUES OF PROFESSIONAL INTEREST

9. What are some issues that interest you professionally? List them as bullets in the space below.

10. What are some things you are professionally curious about? Bullet them below.

11. What are some ideas or practices that you have been pondering? Bullet them below.

12. What are some things that puzzle you professionally? Bullet them below.

LINGERING THOUGHTS

13.   What are some aspects of your professional practice that have caught your attention? Bullet them below.

14.   As you think about your professional practice, what questions have you been thinking about for a long time? List them below.

15.   Which professional practices have appeared successful in your work? List a few that you would like to study and document below.

16.   What professional thoughts keep reoccurring as you do your work? List them below.

Finding My Topic—Part 2

NARROWING APPEALING TOPICS

1. Which discrepancy seems most important and/or interesting to you?

2. Of all of the ways you listed that indicate ways you would like grow, which seems most pressing, worthwhile, and/or exciting?

3. Which of the professional interests that you listed appears most attractive or appealing?

4. Which lingering thought fascinates you the most at this point in time?

5. Which lingering thought troubles you the most at this point in time?

EVALUATING COMMON THEMES

6. What themes keep appearing in part 1 of this frame? List the themes.

7. What theme appears most frequently?

8. What theme do you find most interesting or compelling or worthy at this time?

I think I would like to study . . .

Frame 1.2 FINDING MY TOPIC—PART 2 (continued)

Developing a Thesis Statement

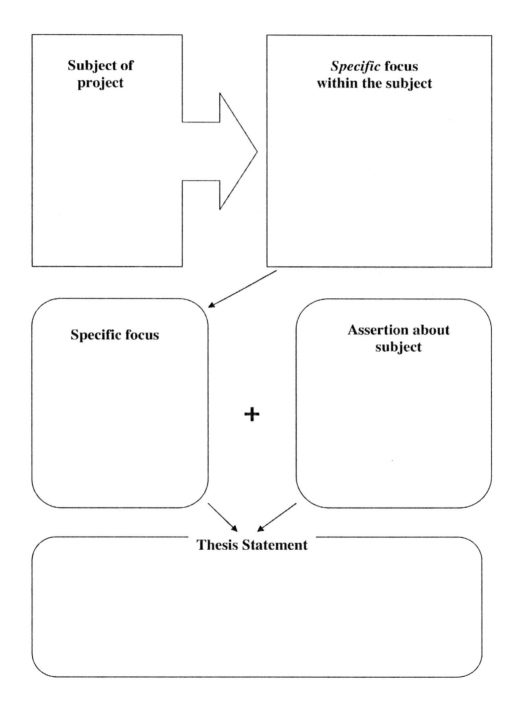

Asking Your Research Question

———— Write the specific topic here. ————

———— How does the specific topic relate to issues in your workplace responsibilities? ————
In this box list as bullets the relationships.

———— What do you want to know about the specific topic? Bullet your thinking here. ————

———— Write your thesis statement. ————

---------------------------------- Write a first draft of your research question(s) here. ----------------------------------

---

Check the research question(s) to make sure you can answer "yes" to each of the items that follow.

1. Is my question narrow enough that I can answer it in the time I have to complete the study? **Yes**   No

2. Am I passionate about finding an answer to the question(s)? **Yes**   No

3. Does the question imply that I will perform actions to find the answer to the question? **Yes**   No

4. Does the question imply that I will collect data to answer the question? **Yes**   No

5. Do I have the freedom to study the question(s)? **Yes**   No

6. Is the question clearly asked? **Yes**   No

7. Can I see a relationship between the research question(s) and the thesis statement? **Yes**   No

If any of the responses above are "no," revise your question(s).

---------------------------------- Write your revised research question(s) here. ----------------------------------

Frame 1.4 ASKING YOUR RESEARCH QUESTION (continued)

Preparing to Discuss the Problems and Context of Your Study

1. What challenges drew you to your topic?

2. What problems surround your topic?

3. Describe the political context of your problem(s). What are the policy issues surrounding your problem?

4. Describe the cultural context of your problem(s).

Frame 1.5 PREPARING TO DISCUSS THE PROBLEMS AND CONTEXT OF YOUR STUDY (continued)

5. Describe the local context of your problem(s).

6. Describe your worksite context of your problem(s).

7. Identify any relevant discussion of your problem in literature.

Describing the Purpose of Your Research

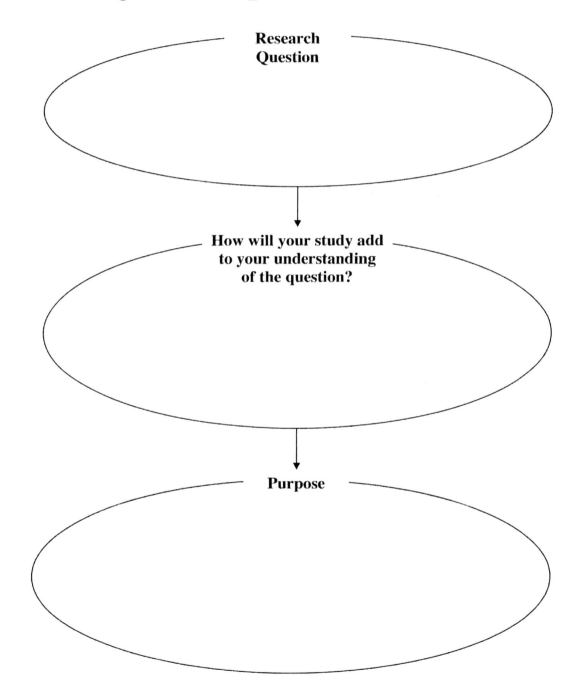

Identifying Related Aspects of Your General Topic—Method 1

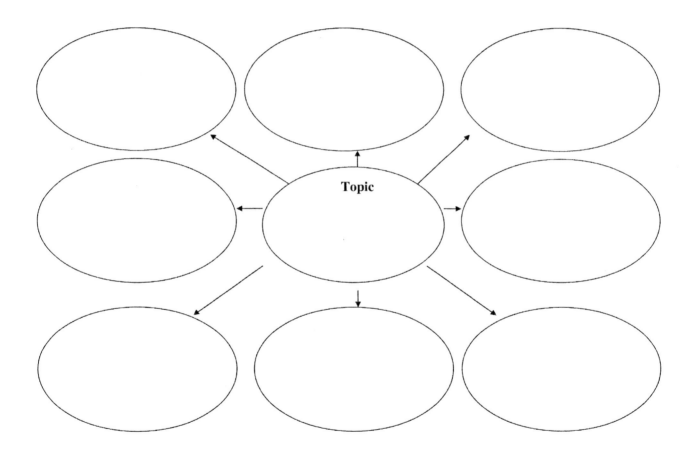

Identifying Related Aspects of Your General Topic—Method 2

1. Cultural issues
   - ➤
   - ➤
   - ➤
   - ➤
   - ➤
   - ➤
   - ➤
   - ➤
   - ➤
   - ➤
   - ➤
   - ➤

2. Development issues
   - ➤
   - ➤
   - ➤
   - ➤
   - ➤
   - ➤
   - ➤
   - ➤
   - ➤
   - ➤
   - ➤

3. Research issues
  ➤
  ➤
  ➤
  ➤
  ➤
  ➤
  ➤
  ➤
  ➤
  ➤
  ➤
  ➤

4. Theory issues
  ➤
  ➤
  ➤
  ➤
  ➤
  ➤
  ➤
  ➤
  ➤
  ➤
  ➤

Frame 1.8 IDENTIFYING RELATED ASPECTS OF YOUR GENERAL TOPIC—METHOD 2 (continued)

5. Practice issues
   ➢
   ➢
   ➢
   ➢
   ➢
   ➢
   ➢
   ➢
   ➢
   ➢
   ➢

6. Concepts issues
   ➢
   ➢
   ➢
   ➢
   ➢
   ➢
   ➢
   ➢
   ➢
   ➢
   ➢

Frame 1.8 IDENTIFYING RELATED ASPECTS OF YOUR GENERAL TOPIC—METHOD 2 (continued)

7. Other issues (for example, policy, key questions, historical perspectives)
   ➢
   ➢
   ➢
   ➢
   ➢
   ➢
   ➢
   ➢
   ➢
   ➢
   ➢
   ➢
   ➢
   ➢
   ➢
   ➢
   ➢
   ➢
   ➢
   ➢
   ➢
   ➢

Frame 1.8 IDENTIFYING RELATED ASPECTS OF YOUR GENERAL TOPIC—METHOD 2 (continued)

Organizing for Writing

1. Write your thesis statement here.

2. Write your research question here.

3. Write your purpose here.

4. Bullet key problems here.

5. Bullet key issues (subtopics) here.

Draw a web that includes items in the above boxes. Examine the web for relationships to help your writing flow from one aspect of the report to the next. Put the thesis statement early in the report. Don't forget a summary/transition paragraph to the review of the literature.

or

Make a traditional outline with the thesis statement early in the outline and end with the transitional thoughts. Example:

I.
    A.
        1.
            a.
            b.
                    and so on

Frame 1.9 ORGANIZING FOR WRITING (continued)

REVIEW OF THE RELATED LITERATURE

The second phase in an action research project is writing a review of the related literature. The review of the literature serves three main purposes. First, it demonstrates your understanding of the field of study. Second, it informs and shapes your action research project. Third, it prepares future readers to better understand the intellectual context of the study.

The literature review usually includes many or all of the components that follow: rationale, historical perspectives and seminal research, key concepts, current research, theoretical perspectives, key debates, and human development. The first component, a rationale for the study, is an important part of the introductory section of your review of the related literature. Frame 2.1, "Writing the Rationale for Your Study," focuses your attention on why your study is important. In the box at the top of the page you will briefly list why your study is worth your time and effort from the perspective of your professional practice. In the box at the bottom of the page you will bullet how the literature would answer the question, "Why bother with this study?" Having established why your study is worthwhile, you are ready to proceed to planning the introduction for this section of your project report.

Often, after discussing the rationale for the study, many researchers will include a historical perspective, where researchers describe the history of the issues and debates surrounding their subject area and the seminal research of the field. Another preliminary element of most discussions is the identification of key concepts in the field. Once the preliminary elements have been

discussed, the researcher can launch into the bulk of the literature review, which is an examination of current research in the field of study. This examination should include a discussion of theoretical perspectives in the field and an identification of key questions or debates in the field. Finally, in many human services studies human development is an important element that needs to conclude the literature review.

Following the rationale frame are a series of frames dedicated to addressing the key elements described in the preceding paragraph. These frames are arranged into four groups. Frame 2.2 will help you prepare to conduct your literature search. The second group of frames, 2.3 through 2.8, will help you keep track of the materials you are studying. Frame 2.9 will help you keep track of important definitions and acronyms. The third group of frames, 2.10 through 2.12, will help you organize the material you have collected in a logical fashion in preparation for writing the review of the related literature. The fourth portion of section 2 is an ethics checklist, Frame 2.13. Each of these frames is discussed in the following paragraphs.

Frame 2.2, "Preparing for the Review of the Related Literature—The Literature Search," is designed to help you get ready to search for articles, books, interviews, and documents that have been published on the subject. The first column of this table is complete. In this column you will find the six typical elements in a literature review: historical perspectives and seminal research; key concepts; current research; theoretical perspectives; key arguments, issues, debates, and questions; and human development issues. You will complete the second and third columns in the frame. In the second column you will consider and then list topics related to each of the six features presented. In the third and final column you will record topic keywords to be used in searching for related literature. Once this table has been completed you are ready to proceed to the literature search itself, using computer databases and libraries.

The second set of frames, Frame 2.3 through Frame 2.8, is designed to help you keep track of the content of the articles, books, interviews, and documents that you are collecting. As you read each piece of literature or study each source, you will complete the frames titled "Research Records—Historical Perspectives and Seminal Research," "Research Records—Key Concepts," "Research Records—Current Research," "Research Records—Theoretical Perspectives," "Research Records—Key Arguments, Issues, Debates, and Questions," and "Research Records—Developmental Issues." In the first column of each table you will record the author's first name, middle initial, and last name. In the second column you will record the publication date of the source. In the third column you will enter the source of the document (journal title, book title, interviewer, website, etc.), the name of the publisher, and the city and state where the publisher is located. In the fourth column you will record the volume and issue number of a journal or the edition of a book. In the fifth column you will note the title of journal articles or chapter titles. In the sixth column you will enter key points and quotes from each source. In the final column record the page number(s) where you have found the information in column six.

By making careful notations in each column you will find organizing your review, citing authorities in your field of study, and preparing your reference page will be much easier. One common and dreaded problem for novice researchers (and sometimes experienced researchers as well) is incomplete or lost records. I have seen many students and a few colleagues despair when they find they can't find a page number for a direct quote or the volume or issue number for a journal.

You may choose to proceed through the frames in the order that they are presented in the book or you may go back and forth between Research Records forms as you study various documents. Depending on the literature review purposes and/or requirements, you may use some or all of the Research Records frames. In other words, the Research Records frames include a variety of subject areas, some of which may not be necessary for individual researchers.

Frame 2.9, "Definitions," was created to help you keep track of acronyms and words that require definition. Again, you will record terms and/or acronyms that require definition as you read the various texts in the review of the literature. In the first column you will record the word to be defined. In the second column you will record any acronym that is used in place of the word you recorded in column one. In the third column you will write the definition or definitions of the word recorded in column one. This third column in the table intentionally says "Definitions," rather than "Definition," because there may be multiple definitions for a term. For example, a term may be defined one way in a dictionary but also may have a unique definition within your profession. On occasion you may find that different authorities define the term in differing ways. Finally, in the fourth column you will record the source (document title, author, publication source and date, page number, chapter number and chapter title, and/or website).

A third set of materials is intended to help you organize in preparation to write your review of the related literature. Three kinds of frames are presented to help with the preparation for writing. These include frames for preparing to write the introduction to your review and frames to help you organize your review of the topics to be discussed.

Frame 2.10, "Preparing to Write the Review of the Related Literature—The Introduction," is designed to assist you in writing the introduction to the review of the related literature. Most researchers will probably want to use this frame because it helps set up the introduction to the review of the literature. In the first box you will write your research question. This will help you stay focused on what to include in the literature review. In the second box you will enter the rationale for your study. In the next box you will jot down any literature that supports your rationale. In the large box in the center of the page you will bullet key points you want to make in your discussion of the literature. Finally, in the last box, write a first draft of the transition to the body of your review of the related literature.

Having planned your introduction to the review, you are ready to organize your thoughts for the body of the review. Two frames, Frame 2.11, "Organizing the Review of the Literature—Linear Option," and Frame 2.12, "Organizing the Review of the Literature—Topic Relationship Option," support two different ways to organize the content of your literature review. You may choose to use either or both of these supports. For example, you may want to complete the first series in Frame 2.11 in order to organize the content around each topic in your review; then, you may wish to complete the topic relationship option in Frame 2.12 to help you order each of the sections you prepared in the linear option.

Frame 2.11, "Organizing the Review of the Literature—Linear Option," provides a space to do a traditional outline of the various components of your literature review. Each of the six boxes is chunked into three areas. The areas are in a chronological form beginning with earliest discussions, moving to following discussions, and ending with current discussions in your area of study. You can record key points under each of the areas on each frame used. Again, you will use only those components that are relevant and/or required in your study. You will need to provide transitions from one component to the next. It is also important to remember that the order in which the components are presented in this text is not necessarily the order in which you will choose to write about each component.

Frame 2.12, "Organizing the Review of the Literature—Topic Relationship Option," is a more graphic way to organize the review of literature. If you use this diagram, you will record key topics in each loop in a logical order. In the last loop you will record thoughts for a transition from the review of the literature to the third section of your action research study: the implementation plan or methodology. Again, this frame can be used in conjunction with or in place of the six linear components from Frame 2.10 and as discussed in the previous paragraph.

Having completed these sets of frames, you are now ready to write your review of the related literature. Once you have written your review of the related literature you will use Frame 2.13, "Writing the Review of the Related Literature—Ethics Checklist." By using this checklist you will ensure that your work is professional and honorable. (See American Educational Research Association and American Psychological Association publications for more information on ethics.)

Writing the Rationale for Your Study

What in your setting makes you think it is important that you do your study?
Why do you think your study is worth your time and effort?

What in the literature explains why your study is important?
How does the literature indicate that your study is worth the bother?

Key points   Sources

Frame 2.2

Preparing for the Review of the Related Literature—The Literature Search

Key Element	Considerations	Keywords
Historical Perspectives / Seminal Research		
Key Concepts		
Current Research		

Theoretical Perspectives		
Key Arguments / Issues / Debates /Questions		
Human Development Issues		

Frame 2.2 PREPARING FOR THE REVIEW OF THE RELATED LITERATURE (continued)

Research Records—Historical Perspectives and Seminal Research

Author	Date	Source, Publisher, City, and State	Volume, Issue	Article Title / Chapter Title	Key Points / Quotes	Pages

Author	Date	Source, Publisher, City, and State	Volume, Issue	Article Title / Chapter Title	Key Points / Quotes	Pages

Frame 2.3 RESEARCH RECORDS—HISTORICAL PERSPECTIVES AND SEMINAL RESEARCH (continued)

Author	Date	Source, Publisher, City, and State	Volume, Issue	Article Title / Chapter Title	Key Points / Quotes	Pages

Frame 2.3 RESEARCH RECORDS—HISTORICAL PERSPECTIVES AND SEMINAL RESEARCH (continued)

Frame 2.4

Research Records—Key Concepts

Author	Date	Source, Publisher, City, and State	Volume, Issue	Article Title / Chapter Title	Key Points / Quotes / Methods	Pages

Author	Date	Source, Publisher, City, and State	Volume, Issue	Article Title / Chapter Title	Key Points / Quotes / Methods	Pages

Frame 2.4 RESEARCH RECORDS—KEY CONCEPTS (continued)

Author	Date	Source, Publisher, City, and State	Volume, Issue	Article Title / Chapter Title	Key Points / Quotes / Methods	Pages

Frame 2.4 RESEARCH RECORDS—KEY CONCEPTS (continued)

Author	Date	Source, Publisher, City, and State	Volume, Issue	Article Title / Chapter Title	Key Points / Quotes / Methods	Pages

Frame 2.4 RESEARCH RECORDS—KEY CONCEPTS (continued)

Research Records—Current Research

Author	Date	Source, Publisher, City, and State	Volume, Issue	Article Title / Chapter Title	Key Points / Quotes	Pages

Author	Date	Source, Publisher, City, and State	Volume, Issue	Article Title / Chapter Title	Key Points / Quotes	Pages

Frame 2.5 RESEARCH RECORDS—CURRENT RESEARCH (continued)

Author	Date	Source, Publisher, City, and State	Volume, Issue	Article Title / Chapter Title	Key Points / Quotes	Pages

Frame 2.5 RESEARCH RECORDS—CURRENT RESEARCH (continued)

Author	Date	Source, Publisher, City, and State	Volume, Issue	Article Title / Chapter Title	Key Points / Quotes	Pages

Frame 2.5 RESEARCH RECORDS—CURRENT RESEARCH (continued)

Author	Date	Source, Publisher, City, and State	Volume, Issue	Article Title / Chapter Title	Key Points / Quotes	Pages

Frame 2.5 RESEARCH RECORDS—CURRENT RESEARCH (continued)

Research Records—Theoretical Perspectives

Author	Date	Source, Publisher, City, and State	Volume, Issue	Article Title / Chapter Title	Key Points / Quotes	Pages

Author	Date	Source, Publisher, City, and State	Volume, Issue	Article Title / Chapter Title	Key Points / Quotes	Pages

Frame 2.6 RESEARCH RECORDS—THEORETICAL PERSPECTIVES (continued)

Author	Date	Source, Publisher, City, and State	Volume, Issue	Article Title / Chapter Title	Key Points / Quotes	Pages

Frame 2.6 RESEARCH RECORDS—THEORETICAL PERSPECTIVES (continued)

Author	Date	Source, Publisher, City, and State	Volume, Issue	Article Title / Chapter Title	Key Points / Quotes	Pages

Frame 2.6 RESEARCH RECORDS—THEORETICAL PERSPECTIVES (continued)

Research Records—Key Arguments, Issues, Debates, and Questions

Author	Date	Source, Publisher, City, and State	Volume, Issue	Article Title / Chapter Title	Key Points / Quotes	Pages

Author	Date	Source, Publisher, City, and State	Volume, Issue	Article Title / Chapter Title	Key Points / Quotes	Pages

Frame 2.7 RESEARCH RECORDS—KEY ARGUMENTS, ISSUES, DEBATES, AND QUESTIONS (continued)

Author	Date	Source, Publisher, City, and State	Volume, Issue	Article Title / Chapter Title	Key Points / Quotes	Pages

Frame 2.7 RESEARCH RECORDS—KEY ARGUMENTS, ISSUES, DEBATES, AND QUESTIONS (continued)

Author	Date	Source, Publisher, City, and State	Volume, Issue	Article Title / Chapter Title	Key Points / Quotes	Pages

Frame 2.7 RESEARCH RECORDS—KEY ARGUMENTS, ISSUES, DEBATES, AND QUESTIONS (continued)

Author	Date	Source, Publisher, City, and State	Volume, Issue	Article Title / Chapter Title	Key Points / Quotes	Pages

Frame 2.7 RESEARCH RECORDS—KEY ARGUMENTS, ISSUES, DEBATES, AND QUESTIONS (continued)

Author	Date	Source, Publisher, City, and State	Volume, Issue	Article Title / Chapter Title	Key Points / Quotes	Pages

Frame 2.7 RESEARCH RECORDS—KEY ARGUMENTS, ISSUES, DEBATES, AND QUESTIONS (continued)

Research Records—Developmental Issues

Author	Date	Source, Publisher, City, and State	Volume, Issue	Article Title / Chapter Title	Key Points / Quotes	Pages

Author	Date	Source, Publisher, City, and State	Volume, Issue	Article Title / Chapter Title	Key Points / Quotes	Pages

Frame 2.8 RESEARCH RECORDS—DEVELOPMENTAL ISSUES (continued)

Author	Date	Source, Publisher, City, and State	Volume, Issue	Article Title / Chapter Title	Key Points / Quotes	Pages

Frame 2.8 RESEARCH RECORDS—DEVELOPMENTAL ISSUES (continued)

Definitions

Term	Acronym	Definitions	Sources

Frame 2.10

Preparing to Write the Review of the Related Literature—The Introduction

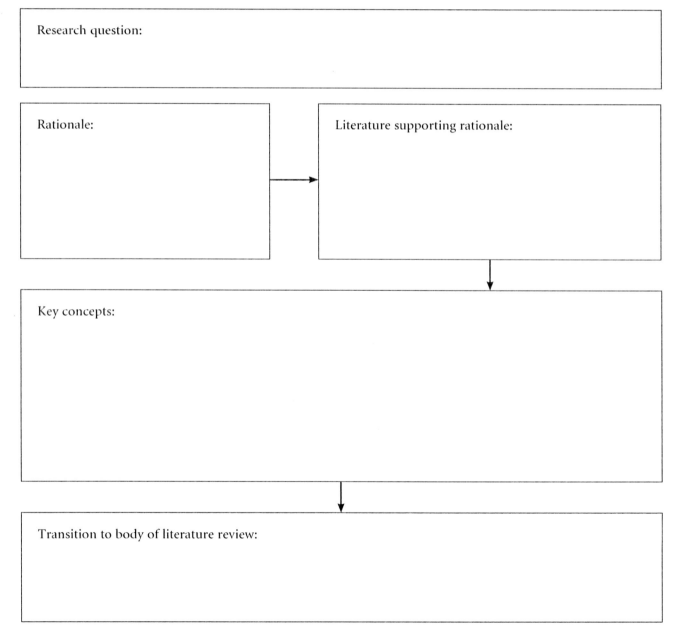

Research question:

Rationale:

Literature supporting rationale:

Key concepts:

Transition to body of literature review:

Organizing the Review of the Literature—Linear Option

I. Key Concepts:*
    A. Earliest Concepts:
        1.
        2.
        3.
        4.
        5.
        6.
        7.
        8.
        9.
       10.

    B. Following Concepts:
        1.
        2.
        3.
        4.
        5.
        6.
        7.
        8.
        9.
       10.
    C. Recent Concepts:
        1.
        2.
        3.
        4.
        5.
        6.
        7.
        8.
        9.
       10.

* Note: You may not have ten items in each section of the literature review. Ten is an arbitrary number. List as many items as you need in each section. This may be more or fewer than ten.

II. Developmental Issues:
   A. Earliest Developmental Issues:
      1.
      2.
      3.
      4.
      5.
      6.
      7.
      8.
      9.
      10.

   B. Following Developmental Issues:
      1.
      2.
      3.
      4.
      5.
      6.
      7.
      8.
      9.
      10.

   C. Recent Developmental Issues:
      1.
      2.
      3.
      4.
      5.
      6.
      7.
      8.
      9.
      10.

Frame 2.11 ORGANIZING THE REVIEW OF THE LITERATURE—LINEAR OPTION (continued)

III. Theoretical Perspectives:
    A. Earliest Perspectives:
        1.
        2.
        3.
        4.
        5.
        6.
        7.
        8.
        9.
        10.

    B. Following Perspectives:
        1.
        2.
        3.
        4.
        5.
        6.
        7.
        8.
        9.
        10.

    C. Recent Perspectives:
        1.
        2.
        3.
        4.
        5.
        6.
        7.
        8.
        9.
        10.

Frame 2.11 ORGANIZING THE REVIEW OF THE LITERATURE—LINEAR OPTION (continued)

IV. Research Studies:
   A. Seminal Studies:
      1.
      2.
      3.
      4.
      5.
      6.
      7.
      8.
      9.
     10.

   B. Following Studies:
      1.
      2.
      3.
      4.
      5.
      6.
      7.
      8.
      9.
     10.

   C. Current Studies:
      1.
      2.
      3.
      4.
      5.
      6.
      7.
      8.
      9.
     10.

Frame 2.11 ORGANIZING THE REVIEW OF THE LITERATURE—LINEAR OPTION (continued)

V. Questions:
    A. Earliest Questions:
        1.
        2.
        3.
        4.
        5.
        6.
        7.
        8.
        9.
        10.

    B. Following Questions:
        1.
        2.
        3.
        4.
        5.
        6.
        7.
        8.
        9.
        10.

    C. Current Questions:
        1.
        2.
        3.
        4.
        5.
        6.
        7.
        8.
        9.
        10.

Frame 2.11 ORGANIZING THE REVIEW OF THE LITERATURE—LINEAR OPTION (continued)

VI. Debates:
    A. Earliest Debates:
        1.
        2.
        3.
        4.
        5.
        6.
        7.
        8.
        9.
        10.

    B. Following Debates:
        1.
        2.
        3.
        4.
        5.
        6.
        7.
        8.
        9.
        10.

    C. Current Debates:
        1.
        2.
        3.
        4.
        5.
        6.
        7.
        8.
        9.
        10.

Frame 2.11 ORGANIZING THE REVIEW OF THE LITERATURE—LINEAR OPTION (continued)

Organizing the Review of the Literature— Topic Relationship Option

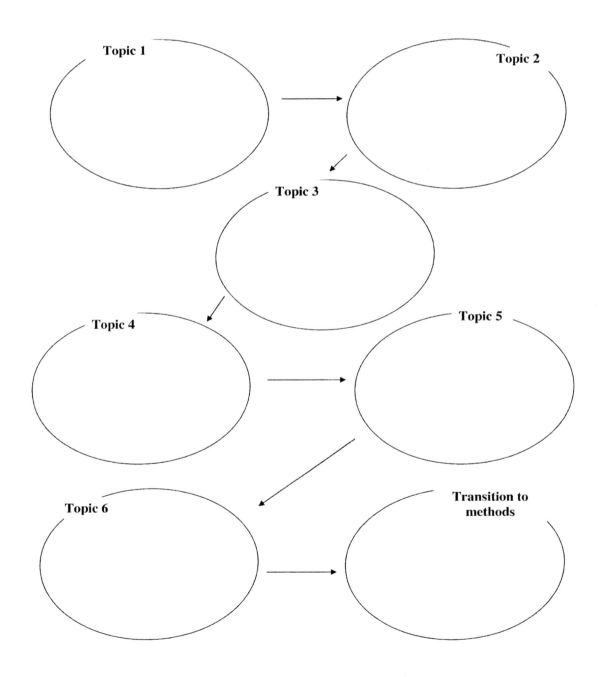

Writing the Review of the Related Literature—Ethics Checklist

Did I . . .	Yes	No	Doesn't Apply
give credit to all authors cited?			
make complete citations?			
make a complete reference page?			
use passages that were long enough to keep their meaning?			
avoid misrepresenting authors' ideas?			
make it clear where authors' voices began and ended?			
avoid gender bias?			
avoid ethnic bias?			
avoid linguistic bias?			
avoid racial bias?			
avoid age bias?			
avoid abilities bias?			
remain culturally sensitive as I wrote my literature review?			

Section 3

METHODOLOGY

The third phase of an action research project is creating an implementation plan. This phase is most often called methodology. The implementation plan is a design plan leading to the generation of data to answer your research question. In other words, section 3 describes the ways in which you will conduct your study. Four main components comprise a methodology: the setting of your study, the procedures and activities you will do to generate data, the data you will collect to answer your research question, and a timeline for activities and data collection. Three components—the setting, the data you will collect, and timeline—are developed in the first part of this section using frames similar to the ones you used in sections 1 and 2. However, the procedures and activities you will do to generate data will vary widely, depending on your topic and available resources. Therefore, the second part of section 3 provides you with forms to use in a variety of circumstances. These are called Data Collection Tools; you will find some very useful, and others you may use only partially or not at all.

METHODOLOGY FRAMES

Frame 3.1, "Describing Your Setting," will help you describe the location for your study and the key characteristics of your location. You will answer each prompt provided as if you were completing a short-answer test. By completing Frame 3.1, you will provide a context for your study.

After completing the first frame, you will find a group of four frames, 3.2 to 3.5, created to help you decide on the procedures and activities you will use to answer your research question. Frame 3.2, "Selecting Actions and Documentation," intends to help you determine key actions and data sources that will help answer your research question. In the first box on this page you will write your research question from Frame 1.4. This will help you remember to create activities and procedures that will provide data to answer your research question. After recording the research question in the first box, you may elect to work across rows to connect individual actions to resulting documentation, or you may choose to list all activities in the first column and then list the resulting documentation in the second column. It doesn't matter whether you list all of the data-generating activities prior to recording data or whether you write one activity and then record the data that activity will generate. Choose the method that seems most logical to you. What is important for you to consider is the connection between the activities and the documentation that the activities will generate in order to answer the research question.

The second frame in this set, Frame 3.3, "Description of Actions," breaks the key actions into a series of critical steps. After listing the key action in column one, you will write the critical steps in completing each action. You will want to include enough detail in the critical steps section to guide you through the activities in a relatively smooth and logical pattern.

Just as the second frame developed details for action steps, the third frame in the group, Frame 3.4, "Description of Documentation Sources," maps out details for data sources. You will list the kinds of documentation that you recorded in the second column from Frame 3.2

in column one of Frame 3.4. In column 2 you will bullet key features of the data source. In the third column you will record how each piece of documentation will help to answer the research question.

The objective of the next frame, "Choosing Sources to Answer Research Question," is provided to help you choose at least three data sources that can be used together to best answer your research question. Before you complete Frame 3.5, you may wish to examine the data collection tools provided at the end of this section. In the triangle in the center of the frame you will record the research question again. Yes, this seems redundant, but it is easy to become so engaged in planning activities that the research question can be forgotten. Recording it again will help you stay focused on the question to be answered. In Frame 3.4 you listed multiple sources of documentation; now in Frame 3.5 you will consider each data source and record the best three data sources in the three boxes provided. In the box at the bottom of the page, you will briefly describe how the three data sources will work together to answer your research question.

Finally, in the last group of forms, three styles of timeline frames are provided. They will help you determine a calendar for orderly implementation. Completing the timeline also will ensure that you have allowed sufficient time to complete all aspects of your project. You should choose the method that you believe is most helpful.

Frame 3.6, "Implementation and Documentation Schedule—Option 1," is a series of calendar pages. You will note key activities and key data collection in the appropriate compartments on each calendar page. You may want to use a pencil to enter this information because it may change your initial thinking as your timeline progresses. Some students have found that working backward from the due date for the project report is easier for them. Other students prefer to proceed from beginning to end of the project. You will use the method that you think will work best for you. Of course, you may not use each calendar page included in Frame 3.6. Some projects will have shorter time limits, while others

will have longer time limits. Multiple calendar pages are included for the study with longer time limits. If you don't like using a calendar to record your ideas, you may want to choose one of the two frames that follow.

Frame 3.7, "Implementation and Documentation Schedule—Option 2," allows you to bullet key activities and documentation by weeks. Of course, you will list key actions and data sources in the order in which they will take place in each week. Again, you may want to use pencil to help you remain flexible while planning. You also have the option either to start at the beginning of the project or to work backward from an ending date. Some students have found it is helpful to them to record key activities with one colored pencil and to record data collection points with a second colored pencil.

The third option for creating a timeline, Frame 3.8, "Implementation and Documentation Schedule—Option 3," is a traditional linear timeline, where you will write key dates above a line of arrows and the related activities across the line of arrows beneath the line. Some investigators prefer to work backward on the timeline. Others prefer to work from the beginning of the timeline to the end of the timeline. Still others prefer to work back and forth along the timeline. What is important is that you don't run out of time when implementing the project. Carefully planning your timeline will help you to implement your project in a timely and logical manner.

The last frame in the planning portion of section 3 is Frame 3.9, "Planning and Data Collection—Ethics Checklist." This form is based on professional research guidelines from the American Psychological Association and the American Educational Research Association and guidelines that make sense in behaving in a respectful, responsible, professional manner. (For a detailed discussion of these professional guidelines visit the American Psychological Association and American Educational Research Association websites.) The checklist can be used as you plan your study and then reused after you have written a draft of your methodology report. By reusing the checklist you will ensure that you have planned to proceed in a principled way. You will have protected your participants and yourself.

DATA COLLECTION TOOLS

In the second part of section 3 you will find twenty-one data collection frames. Although these forms are varied and are offered to help you select data collection tools, they are far from the only tools that are appropriate and beneficial to action researchers. Before you consider the frames, consider some other ways of documenting your actions, such as work samples and taping. Having considered kinds of data to collect without the use of frames, it is now time to study and select any frames that will be useful for data collection.

The first frame, Data Collection Tool 3.1, "Interview Protocol Form," was designed to assist you in developing an effective and efficient method of asking guided questions to someone. A well-developed interview protocol leads to answering your research question. A poorly designed protocol may give you little or no data to answer your research question. This form provides the framework for developing a strong protocol. It is important to complete the preliminary items—the interviewee's name, the date, location, and time of the interview—in the protocol prior to the interview. Researchers often think they will remember these details and find that in reality they forget them or remember them incorrectly. You may want to make shorthand symbols before the interview, but if you find yourself using symbols or abbreviations during the interview, record them then.

The body of the interview protocol follows the preliminary items. It consists of a space for your question, a space for the interviewee's answer, a space to write a probe, and a place to record the interviewee's response to the probe. Two of the spaces, the question and the probe spaces, are briefly discussed below.

Because it is important to keep the interview short and focused, this protocol contains space for only ten questions. You may choose to use more or fewer items in your protocol. Think about each question carefully, making sure it answers your research question. Often open-ended questions generate more data than questions requiring one-word answers. That does not mean there is never a time for questions soliciting one-word answers.

After you have written your questions, it is time to consider probes. Probes or prompts are questions or statements that encourage interviewees to elaborate on their response to the question. Some typical probes are as follow:

What makes you say that?
Tell me a story about when that happened.
Why do you say that?
Please give me an example of that.
Tell me more about that.

After you have considered probes, record one for each question. You never know when you might encounter someone who needs a little help giving complete answers.

It is helpful to capture full quotes. Be as exact as you can in recording responses. If you miss a part or cannot keep up with the interviewee, tell them you can't keep up with all their good ideas and ask them to repeat or slow down. If you encounter an interviewee who gives you information that does not relate to your study, you do not have to record everything she or he says.

Finally, don't forget to thank the interviewees for their time and willingness to share their thoughts, and let them know you will be happy to share the results of your study when it is complete.

The second tool, Data Collection Tool 3.2, "Preparation Checklist for an Interview," is provided to make sure you are well prepared for successful interview sessions. Upon completing your preparation for your interviews, read through and check yes or no to answer the questions. After you have completed the checklist, use what you have discovered to help you prepare for the interview, revise your protocol, practice interviewing and recording, and follow up the interview.

Data Collection Tool 3.3, "Time Sampling Form," can be used to help you record how often something happens. It also can help you identify time patterns of events or behaviors. Again, prior to watching for events or behaviors, it is important to complete the preliminary information: occurrence to be observed, date, and setting. In the recording key box you can note any symbols you use in recording. You may use something as simple as a hash mark. You may need to use something more specific, such as A = attending to task and N = not attending to task. Use whatever symbols make sense to you and help you answer your research question.

After completing the preliminary part of the form, you will need to complete two other parts of the form. You will want to record in the first column the name of the individual or individuals whom you wish to observe. In the second column, the unit of time column, you will need to write the observation times, using equal intervals of time. The length of the interval will depend upon what you are attempting to capture. After you have entered the times that you will be checking for the behavior or event, you are ready to use the checklist. In addition to recording when and/or how often events or behaviors occur, you may wish to make notes in the notes column.

The fourth tool, Data Collection Tool 3.4, "Individual Event Sampling Form," helps you keep track of events that relate to one individual. Here you are not so concerned with time. You want to know if and how often events occur. After completing the preliminary items on the form, you will enter the activities you wish to observe. After you have entered that information, you are ready to use the body of the recording table. Again, you can tally how many events occur in each column and make notes in the note column.

Data Collection Tool 3.5, "Group Event Sampling Form," serves much the same purpose as the individual event sampling form. In this form you are able to observe actions by multiple study participants. After completing the preliminary items on the form, you will enter the activities you wish to observe and the names of the participants you wish to observe. After you have entered that information, you are ready to use the body of the recording table. Again, you can tally how many events occur in each column and make notes in the note column.

"Group Skills Checklist," Data Collection Tool 3.6, helps you make note of who has attained skills and to what extent they have attained each skill. The attainment key box is a place for you to record your coding system. You may choose just to make a check if the skill is attained. You can also record partial attainment. For example, you might make the following notes in the attainment key box: M = mastery, D = developing, F = failing to approach mastery, and N = not observed. The last notation recognizes that the skill may not have been displayed while you were observing but may be displayed in another setting. Again, after completing the preliminary items and recording names and skills, you are ready to begin collecting data.

Data Collection Tool 3.7, "Individual Skills Checklist," is much like the group skills checklist, except that it is used with just one test subject. Again, you will record the preliminary items on the frame and then list the skills you wish to monitor in the skills column prior to using the form. Once you have completed that, you are able to begin collecting data.

"Field Notes," Data Collection Tool 3.8, provides you with a place to record happenings related to your research question. Again, the date, time, and setting are important because they may help you discover patterns or trends. The first column on this frame is for recording, without judgment or interpretation, things you perceive with your senses. The second column is a place to write your impressions, interpretations, and thoughts.

Data Collection Tool 3.9, "Professional Journal," is much like the field notes frame. It provides the opportunity to record your thoughts and then make inferences from them. Many students report that taking a few minutes at the end of the day to record their thoughts was helpful as they implemented their studies.

The tenth data collection tool, 3.10, provided in this section is the professional log. The professional log is related to the professional journal. A log typically has shorter entries than a journal. It is a place to quickly jot down ideas.

Data Collection Tool 3.11, "Anecdotal Notes Form," looks similar to the professional log, but its intent is different. Whereas the log is a place to capture thoughts and ideas, the anecdotal notes form is a place to capture actual events or direct observations. Initially, it is only the event or observed behavior that you are attempting to capture. Just as in the recording of field notes, impressions, interpretations, and judgments are separated from the actual observations. After completing the preliminary lines of the tool you are ready to record your observations. Notice that the first column says "Name(s)." On one hand, it may be important to your study to focus on one study participant. On the other hand, it may be more useful to your study to attend to the behaviors of multiple participants and their interactions. The final column remains a place for your thoughts.

Data Collection Tool 3.12, "Sociogram," is another way to describe participants' interactions. As in all of the observational tools, recording the date, time, and setting is an important initial step in your observation. In the sociogram, you will write initials of participants in the circles provided. You will then add connector lines between participants' circles to indicate interactions. By adding an arrow to the connector lines you can indicate the origin and direction of the interaction. It is possible to note different kinds of interactions by using multiple kinds of paths, but it is often difficult for a beginner to record multiple kinds of interactions as quickly as they happen. Making a key to initials and connector lines can be done before the observation or quickly after the observation. A key for connector lines might be something like the one shown at the bottom of Figure 3.1.

The next tool is a photo log. You may be able to record the date and photo number on a digital camera. If your camera doesn't have a date and photo number identification system, you will want to record that information in Data Collection Tool 3.13. As you examine your photos to determine which photos help answer your research question, it will be helpful to record a possible caption for each photo. This will help you remember why you chose each photo.

The next two data collection tools are specific to research involving reading and comprehension. Data Collection Tool 3.14, "Running Records Form," helps teachers keep track of reading mistakes children make during a diagnostic procedure called miscue analysis. Miscue analysis is a method to study the errors a child makes in an oral reading. Errors include a correction,

an insertion, an omission, a reversal, a repetition, and a substitution. (See Clay, 2000, for more information on running records and miscue analysis.) In the initial lines of this frame, you will record the student's name, date of record, the stop and start times of the observation, the title of the text, whether the text is a new text or a text the child has previously read, the type of text (reading series or trade book, for example), who selected the book (you or the child), the length of the passage the student read, and the reading level of the book, if it is leveled. During the reading you will record, using your own shorthand system, the child's miscues, such as substitutions, omissions, long pauses, repetitions, self-corrections, or insertions. In the next column there is a space to record assistance in reading the passage, such as the child's request for help or prompts or cues you provide for the child. The third column provides a space to record the page and paragraph number where the miscue or prompt occurred. The child's approach to the passage may be recorded in the fourth column. In this space you can record any signs of discomfort or any distractions or other events influencing the reading. In the fifth column you will write your inferences. The sixth and final column is a place for you to add another feature you wish to record. Don't forget to write what that feature is at the top of the column.

Data Collection Tool 3.15, "Retelling Form," begins with information to complete prior to the retelling. As the retelling begins, you will make note of each item that has been included in the retelling and record any additional observations about each item in the appropriate columns. The final portion of this form, "Teacher Notes," is a place to add your thoughts about the retelling.

The sixteenth data collection tool, 3.16, is a checklist to help you in the development of forced-choice data collection tools, which are often used in questionnaires and surveys. The next three data collection tools are forced-choice questionnaires. Forced-choice forms can include Likert-type scales, open-ended question forms, or multiple-choice forms, including those with a yes/no choice. You may have seen questionnaires or surveys that have used a combination of these methods. Prior to using the checklist, you will want to consider the

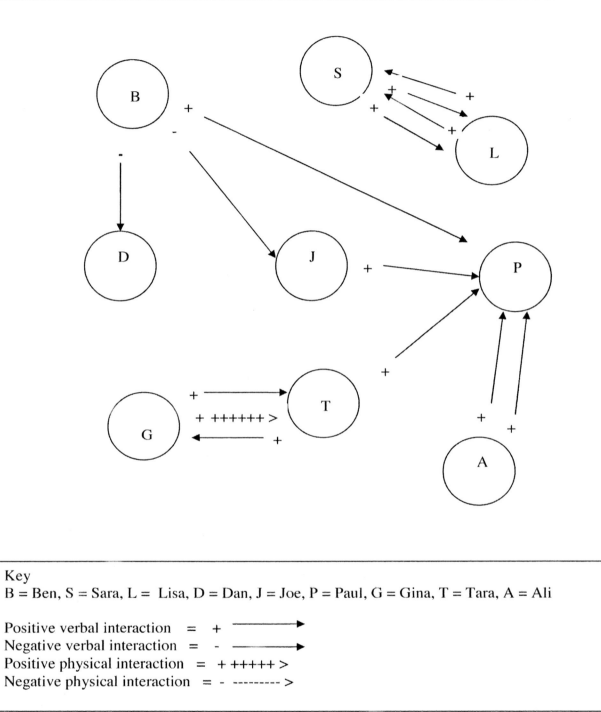

Key
B = Ben, S = Sara, L = Lisa, D = Dan, J = Joe, P = Paul, G = Gina, T = Tara, A = Ali

Positive verbal interaction   =   + ⟶
Negative verbal interaction   =   - ⟶
Positive physical interaction   =   + +++++ >
Negative physical interaction   =   - --------- >

Figure 3.1. Sample Sociogram with Key Children's Social Interactions

purpose of the form, who will complete the form, how the form will be distributed, and who will distribute it.

The checklist is provided to assist you in evaluating your data collection tool prior to its actual use. Again, this is important because without evaluating and testing out your tool you may fail to get helpful data. Upon drafting your forced-choice data collection tool, read through the checklist and check yes or no to answer the questions. After you have completed the checklist, use what you have discovered to help you revise your form. After revisions are made, it would be helpful to test it out on a few people who will not be participants in your study. Their responses might provide you with insights to further sharpen your data collection tool. After your final revisions you are ready to distribute the form.

On the data collection tools there are spaces provided for name and date. Often, in order to protect the confidentiality of respondents, names are not provided by the participants. Sometimes participants are assigned numbers or pseudonyms to write in the name space. This is useful if you are planning to do a pre- and post-event ranking. If this is the case, you will ask respondents to record the number or pseudonym to make sure they don't forget it when you want to do the post-event ranking. You may or may not have groups in your study. If you are using one group, you will not need to complete the group portion of these tools. In other words, the task on questionnaires and surveys is to find a balance between getting the information that you truly need and protecting the respondents' identities. Protecting the respondents' identities is not only ethically correct, it also enhances the chances that the respondents will give more honest answers.

Data Collection Tool 3.17, "Likert-Type Scale," is an example of a forced-choice tool. The frame forces your participants to select responses to a stem, a sentence, or a phrase that you want them to consider. You have probably completed many Likert-type scales. For example, you may have been asked to complete a question such as the one that follows. "To what extent do you agree with the following statement: I like to read."

4—very much
3—quite a bit
2—a little
1—not at all

The number of responses provided on forced-choice tools varies from scale to scale. One advantage to the four-point scale such as the one above is that it doesn't allow your participants to "sit on the fence." The scale doesn't have a midpoint, which can be a place that some participants select to soften their responses or to avoid making a commitment to a point of view. Each numerical point will have a statement attached to it. For example, you often will see choices such as this:

1—strongly disagree
2—disagree
3—agree
4—strongly agree

You will clearly describe the comments that are attached to each numeral in your directions to your participants. The directions for completing your scale are important because your participants may not have a chance to ask you for clarification.

Another feature of the scale provided in Data Collection Tool 3.17 is that each stem and response space is followed by a probe. On the scale provided it is called "follow up." The follow-up space asks your participants to elaborate on their forced numerical choice. Sample follow-up statements and questions may include the following:

What makes you choose that number?
Tell me a story that is an example of why you chose the number that you did.
Why did you choose the number that you did?
Tell me about why you chose the number that you did.
Please explain your choice.

(See Duckworth, 1973, for more information on designing questionnaires.)

Another type of forced-choice tool is a form in which the respondent has to rank items. Ranking tools often ask people to rate items from less to most important, from best to worst, or from most favored to least favored. You are asking your participants to evaluate events, ideas, concepts, behaviors, or values and then rank the items. You will need to consider the issues of confidentiality and critical data, just as you would if you chose a Likert-type scale. You will also have to write clear and concise directions.

Data Collection Tool 3.18, "Ranking Form I," is an example of a forced-choice ranking form. Just as the name of the tool implies, you are forcing your participants to rank items. At the top of the form, there is space provided for name, date, and group. You may or may not have groups in your study. If you are using one group, you will not need to complete this space. You will need to write clear, concise directions to your participants. Following the directions, you will list the items that you want them to rank. The final space on the form has a list of numbers. This is the place the participants will write their ranking.

Data Collection Tool 3.19, "Ranking Form II," is another example of a forced-choice tool. With this form, you provide a list of items down the left side of the page. After each item is a blank line, and the student writes in the ranking number on the blank line.

Data Collection Tool 3.20, "Open-Ended Question Form," is not a forced-choice tool. This tool provides a format to record open-ended questions. After recording the preliminary lines of the form, as appropriate, you will write a carefully worded set of directions. In the space that follows, you will write questions and leave space for responses. Although this form has spaces for eight questions, you may have more or fewer than eight questions. Again, it is important to ask as few questions as possible and still have your question answered.

The last tool provided, Data Collection Tool 3.21, "Multiple-Choice Form," is the final questionnaire frame. After completing the preliminary lines, as necessary and as appropriate, you will write a concise and clear set of directions. Following the directions, you will write your stems, which are statements or queries to help you answer your research question. After the stem, you will construct between three to five response choices. You may choose to have fewer than five responses. You may have seen humorous or silly response choices on multiple-choice exams. On a questionnaire, silly or funny choices are inappropriate. They waste your respondents' time and may make it appear that you don't take your own study seriously. Therefore, you will carefully construct response choices in a serious manner.

Before you formalize your methodology it important to make sure you are proceeding in a professional manner. The ethical checklist presented in Frame 3.10 as the final frame in section 3 will help you monitor ethical considerations. After completing the checklist, make any necessary adjustments to your methodology. (See American Educational Research Association and American Psychological Association publications for more information on ethics.)

Now that you have decided which tools you will use to collect data and manage your data, you are ready to implement your plan and begin collecting data.

Describing Your Setting

DESCRIBING THE SETTING

1. Describe the geographic location where you will implement your study. Bullet key points below. (Do not name your worksite or district.)

2. List key components of workplace policy and practices guidelines.

3. List the mission, philosophy, or belief statement(s) of the organization.

4. List key demographic information for implementation site.

   Examples: (a) number of people in the study, (b) ages of study participants, (c) grade level(s), (d) socioeconomic data about the community, (e) educational level of community, (f) gender breakdown of participants in study, and (g) how and why you selected participants.

5. List key curriculum and instruction features that relate to your study.

6. What is the general timeframe for the study?

   a. time in the academic year

   b. significant events in the setting at the time of the study

Dates:

From _____ through _____

Frame 3.1 DESCRIBING YOUR SETTING (continued)

Selecting Actions and Documentation

Research Question:

What kind of activities and resulting documents, artifacts, or data would help answer your research question? Bullet them below.

Key Actions	Resulting Documentation

Frame 3.3

Description of Actions

Key Action	Critical Steps in Action

Frame 3.4

Description of Documentation Sources

Kind of document, artifact, or data	Description of document, artifact, or data	How document, artifact, or data would answer the research question

Choosing Sources to Answer Research Question

Choose the three kinds of documentation that will best answer your research question. Write those in the boxes below.

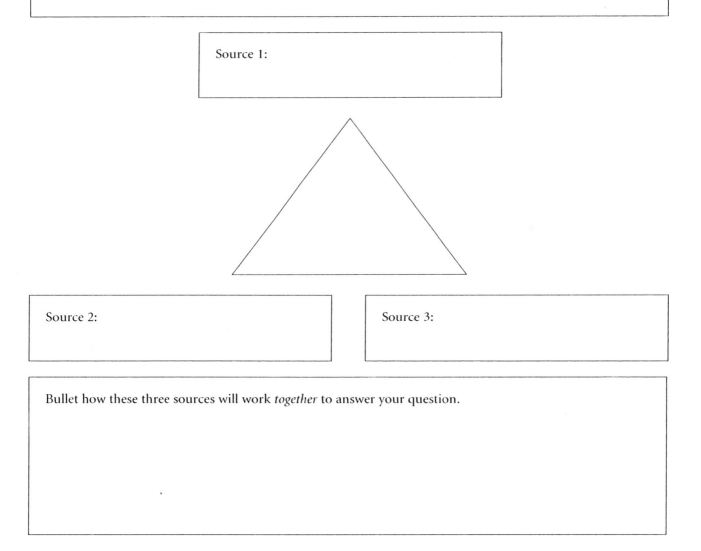

Source 1:

Source 2:

Source 3:

Bullet how these three sources will work *together* to answer your question.

Implementation and Documentation Schedule—Option 1

Weeks _____

Sunday	Monday	Tuesday	Wednesday	Thursday	Friday	Saturday

Weeks _____

Sunday	Monday	Tuesday	Wednesday	Thursday	Friday	Saturday

Frame 3.6 IMPLEMENTATION AND DOCUMENTATION SCHEDULE—OPTION 1 (continued)

Weeks _____

Sunday	Monday	Tuesday	Wednesday	Thursday	Friday	Saturday

Frame 3.6 IMPLEMENTATION AND DOCUMENTATION SCHEDULE—OPTION 1 (continued)

Weeks _____

Sunday	Monday	Tuesday	Wednesday	Thursday	Friday	Saturday

Frame 3.6 IMPLEMENTATION AND DOCUMENTATION SCHEDULE—OPTION 1 (continued)

Implementation and Documentation Schedule—Option 2

Week 1

Key Activities:

-
-
-
-
-

Key Documentation:

-
-
-
-
-
-
-
-
-
-
-
-

Week 2

Key Activities:

-
-
-
-
-
-
-

Key Documentation:

-
-
-
-
-
-
-
-
-
-
-
-
-
-
-

Frame 3.7 IMPLEMENTATION AND DOCUMENTATION SCHEDULE—OPTION 2 (continued)

Week 3

Key Activities:

-
-
-
-
-
-
-

Key Documentation:

-
-
-
-
-
-
-
-
-
-
-
-
-
-
-

Frame 3.7 IMPLEMENTATION AND DOCUMENTATION SCHEDULE—OPTION 2 (continued)

Week 4

    Key Activities:

-
-
-
-
-
-
-

    Key Documentation:

-
-
-
-
-
-
-
-
-
-
-
-
-
-

Frame 3.7 IMPLEMENTATION AND DOCUMENTATION SCHEDULE—OPTION 2 (continued)

Week 5

Key Activities:

-
-
-
-
-
-
-

Key Documentation:

-
-
-
-
-
-
-
-
-
-
-
-
-
-

Frame 3.7 IMPLEMENTATION AND DOCUMENTATION SCHEDULE—OPTION 2 (continued)

Week 6

Key Activities:

-
-
-
-
-
-
-

Key Documentation:

-
-
-
-
-
-
-
-
-
-
-
-
-
-
-

Frame 3.7 IMPLEMENTATION AND DOCUMENTATION SCHEDULE—OPTION 2 (continued)

Week 7

Key Activities:

-
-
-
-
-
-
-

Key Documentation:

-
-
-
-
-
-
-
-
-
-
-
-
-
-

Frame 3.7 IMPLEMENTATION AND DOCUMENTATION SCHEDULE—OPTION 2 (continued)

Week 8

Key Activities:

-
-
-
-
-
-
-

Key Documentation:

-
-
-
-
-
-
-
-
-
-
-
-
-
-
-

Frame 3.7 IMPLEMENTATION AND DOCUMENTATION SCHEDULE—OPTION 2 (continued)

Implementation and Documentation Schedule—Option 3

Dates

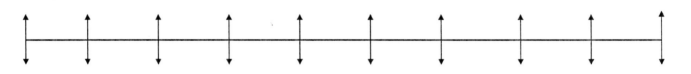

Action and Documentation

Note: You may want to make actions and documentation sources in different colors.

Dates

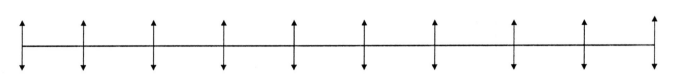

Action and Documentation

Frame 3.8 IMPLEMENTATION AND DOCUMENTATION SCHEDULE—OPTION 3 (continued)

Dates

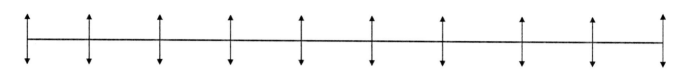

Action and Documentation

Dates

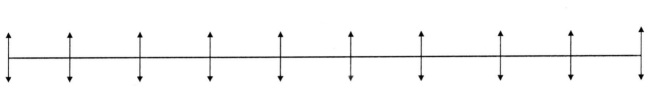

Action and Documentation

Frame 3.8 IMPLEMENTATION AND DOCUMENTATION SCHEDULE—OPTION 3 (continued)

Dates

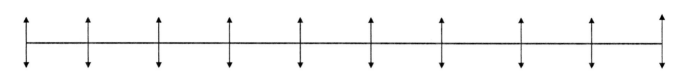

Action and Documentation

Dates

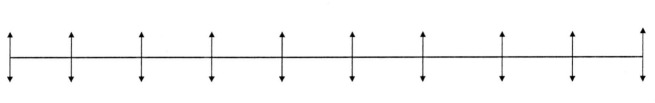

Action and Documentation

Frame 3.8 IMPLEMENTATION AND DOCUMENTATION SCHEDULE—OPTION 3 (continued)

Planning and Data Collection— Ethics Checklist

Did I . . .	Yes	No	Doesn't Apply
let my institution know about my research plans?			
let my institution know the purpose of my study?			
follow my institution's policies and guidelines in my plan?			
consider my institution's calendar and activities?			
protect the identity of my institution when necessary?			
avoid jargon or technical language, communicating in a clear simple manner?			
consider participants' English speaking ability, providing translators as necessary?			
let parents know the purpose of my study?			
let guardians know that their child does not have to participate?			
let guardians know that their child won't be punished for not participating?			
let guardians know of any rewards or benefits and/or risks for their child?			
let guardians know their child can withdraw from my study at any time?			
have children assent to their participation using age and culturally appropriate language?			
protect my participants' identity?			
let my participants know that I'll do my best to protect their identity?			
tell my participants what I will do if their identity is compromised?			
tell my participants that they did not have to participate?			
let participants know that they will not be punished for not participating?			
let participants know of any rewards or benefits related to the study?			

Did I . . .	Yes	No	Doesn't Apply
keep any financial incentives to a minimum, if provided at all?			
do all I could to protect my participants, socially, physically, emotionally, and mentally?			
let participants know they can withdraw at any time?			
tell participants about any risks involved with the study?			
plan to attend to any cultural considerations related to the participants?			
consider my own cultural biases, perceptions, values, attitudes, and beliefs in planning?			
consider linguistic differences between myself and my participants?			
plan to use culturally responsive actions in my activities?			
ask only absolutely necessary personal information?			
inform my participants or their parents that I will share with them the findings from my study?			

Frame 3.9 PLANNING AND DATA COLLECTION—ETHICS CHECKLIST (continued)

Interview Protocol Form

Name: _____   Date: _____

Location: _____   Time: _____

Setting:

Shorthand symbols:

Greeting:

Question 1:

Response:

Probe:

Response:

Question 2:

Response:

Probe:

Response:

Question 3:

Response:

Probe:

Response:

Data Collection Tool 3.1. INTERVIEW PROTOCOL FORM (continued)

Question 4:

Response:

Probe:

Response:

Question 5:

Response:

Probe:

Response:

Data Collection Tool 3.1. INTERVIEW PROTOCOL FORM (continued)

Question 6:

Response:

Probe:

Response:

Question 7:

Response:

Probe:

Response:

Data Collection Tool 3.1. INTERVIEW PROTOCOL FORM (continued)

Question 8:

Response:

Probe:

Response:

Question 9:

Response:

Probe:

Response:

Data Collection Tool 3.1. INTERVIEW PROTOCOL FORM (continued)

Question 10:

Response:

Probe:

Response:

Thank you statement:

Data Collection Tool 3.1. INTERVIEW PROTOCOL FORM (continued)

Preparation Checklist for an Interview

	Yes	No
1. Did my scheduling of the interview include the following items?		
a. date for the interview	___	___
b. time for the interview	___	___
c. specific location for the interview	___	___
d. statement about the purpose of my study	___	___
e. statement about voluntary nature of the interview	___	___
f. statement about benefits of the interview	___	___
g. statement of confidentiality	___	___
h. thank you to the tentative interviewee	___	___

	Yes	No
2. What will I use to record the interview?		
a. tape recorder	___	___
1. Are my questions ready for use?	___	___
2. Do I have probes planned?	___	___
3. Do I have back-up tapes?	___	___
4. Do I have back-up batteries?	___	___
5. Have I tested the recorder and its settings?	___	___
6. Have I practiced using the device?	___	___
7. Have I informed the interviewee about taping?	___	___
8. Am I prepared to translate the tapes?	___	___
9. Do I have a back-up tape recorder?	___	___

	Yes	No
b. video camera	——	——
1. Are my questions ready for use?	——	——
2. Do I have probes planned?	——	——
3. Do I have a back-up camera?	——	——
4. Do I have any power cables I may need?	——	——
5. Have I tested the camera and its settings?	——	——
6. Have I practiced using the device?	——	——
7. Have I informed the interviewee about it?	——	——
8. Am I prepared to translate the video?	——	——

	Yes	No
c. printed interview protocol	——	——
1. Is it formatted for easy use?	——	——
2. Is there enough space to record responses?	——	——
3. Do I have probes in place?	——	——
4. Is there enough space for probe responses?	——	——
5. Do I have more than one writing tool?	——	——
6. Will I use a clipboard?	——	——
7. Have I informed the interviewee about writing?	——	——

Data Collection Tool 3.2. PREPARATION CHECKLIST FOR AN INTERVIEW (continued)

3. Is my interview protocol well developed?   Yes   No

   a. Does it include a way to establish rapport?   _____   _____

   b. Does it stick to my research topic?   _____   _____

   c. Do I have effective probes planned?   _____   _____

   d. Is it formatted for easy use?   _____   _____

   e. Will it help me answer my research question?   _____   _____

   f. Does my interview say I will share study results?   _____   _____

   g. Does my interview restate confidentiality promises? _____   _____

   h. Does it include a thank you to the interviewee?   _____   _____

4. How did my practice interview work?   Yes   No

   a. Did the practice interview run smoothly?   _____   _____

     If not, what changes will I make? _____

     _____

   b. Was the interview too long?   _____   _____

     Is so, how I will shorten it? _____

     _____

   c. Did my recording method work well?   _____   _____

     If not, how will I adjust my methods? _____

     _____

   d. What other changes do I need to make? _____

     _____

5. Have I completed my interview follow up?   Yes   No

   a. Did I thank the interviewee in writing?   _____   _____

   b. Did I share the results of my study as promised?   _____   _____

Data Collection Tool 3.2. PREPARATION CHECKLIST FOR AN INTERVIEW (continued)

Time Sampling Form

Occurrence to be observed: _____ Date: _____

Setting: _____

_____

Recording key

Name	Unit of Time						Notes

Individual Event Sampling Form

Name: _____   Activity to be observed: _____ -

Setting: _____

_____

Key for other activities

Date	Time	Activity 1	Activity 2	Activity 3	Other Activities	Notes

Group Event Sampling Form

Date: _____   Activity to be observed: _____

Setting: _____

_____

Key for other activities

Name	Time	Activity 1	Activity 2	Activity 3	Other Activities	Notes

Group Skills Checklist

Setting:_____

_____

Date: _____   Time: _____

Attainment Key

Name	Skill 1	Skill 2	Skill 3	Notes

Individual Skills Checklist

Name: _____ Date: _____ Time: _____

Setting:_____

_____

Skill	Fully Attained	Partially Attained	Not Attained	Notes

Field Notes

Date: _____   Time: _____

Setting: _____

_____

Observations	Notes to Self

Professional Journal

Date: _____   Time: _____

Entry—My Thoughts	Inferences

Professional Log

Date: _____   Time: _____

Setting:_____

_____

Notes	Interpretation

Date: _____   Time: _____

Setting:_____

_____

Notes	Interpretation

Anecdotal Notes Form

Date: _____   Time: _____

Setting:_____

_____

Name	Observed Behavior	Interpretations

Date: _____   Time: _____

Setting:_____

_____

Name	Observed Behavior	Interpretations

Sociogram

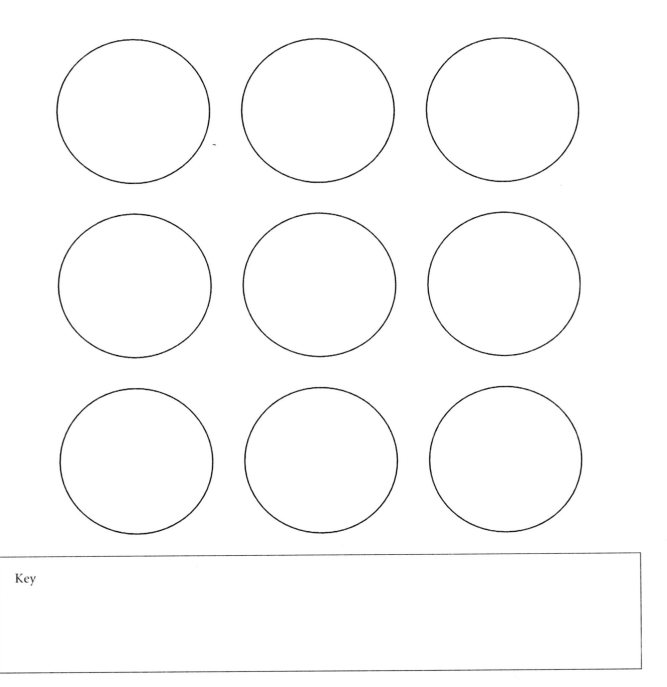

Key

Photo Log

Photo Number/I.D.	Date	Possible Caption

Running Records Form

Name: _____ Date: _____ Time: _____

Text Title: _____

_____ Familiar Text _____ Unfamiliar Text   Type of Text: _____

Selected by: _____ Number of Words: _____ Level: _____

Miscues	Prompts	Page/ Paragraph	Approach to Text	Inferences	Other

Retelling Form

Name: _____   Date: _____   Time: _____

Text Title: _____

Setting:_____

_____

Includes Beginning	Includes Ending	Includes Plot Details	Includes Character Details	Uses Story Sequence

Teacher Notes:

Data Collection Tool 3.16

Forced-Choice Checklist

Have I . . .

	Yes	No
included only one topic per question?		
avoided wordiness?		
avoided negative wording?		
avoided bias in my wording?		
used simple and appropriate language, avoided jargon?		
used gender-neutral terms?		
used proper grammar?		
avoided extreme wording (such as "always" or "never")?		
followed a logical order?		
considered the well-being of my participants? Are personal questions necessary?		
included only necessary items?		
carefully considered definition of terms?		
included all necessary items?		
considered if the item will get the information I need?		
asked "an expert" to review it and make comments or use standards as a content base?		
checked to make sure it is easy to complete?		
checked to make sure my directions are clear?		
kept it as short as possible?		
kept the format neat and uncluttered?		
checked to make sure the form can be used consistently?		
said thank you?		

Likert-Type Scale

Name: _____ Date: _____

Directions:

Question 1:

Follow-up 1:

Question 2:

1   2   3   4

Follow-up 2:

Question 3:

```
1                    2                    3                    4
|────────────────────|────────────────────|────────────────────|
|                    |                    |                    |
```

Follow-up 3:

Question 4:

```
1                    2                    3                    4
|────────────────────|────────────────────|────────────────────|
|                    |                    |                    |
```

Follow-up 4:

Question 5:

1   2   3   4

Follow-up 5:

Question 6:

1   2   3   4

Follow-up 6:

Data Collection Tool 3.17. LIKERT-TYPE SCALE (continued)

Question 7:

Follow-up 7:

Question 8:

1   2   3   4

Follow-up 8:

Data Collection Tool 3.17. LIKERT-TYPE SCALE (continued)

Question 9:

Follow-up 9:

Question 10:

1   2   3   4

Follow-up 10:

Thank you for completing this form. Your thoughts and time are appreciated.

Data Collection Tool 3.17. LIKERT-TYPE SCALE (continued)

Ranking Form I

Name: _____   Date: _____

Group: _____

Directions:

Items to rank:

1.

2.

3.

4.

5.

6.

7.

8.

9.

10.

Thank you for your honest responses.

Ranking Form II

Name: _____ Date: _____

Group: _____

Directions:

Item   Rank:

_____

_____

_____

_____

_____

_____

_____

Thank you for your honest responses.

Open-Ended Question Form

Name: _____   Date: _____

Group: _____

Directions:

Questions:

1.

2.

3.

4.

5.

6.

7.

8.

Thank you for answering these questions.

Multiple-Choice Form

Name: _____ Date: _____

Group: _____

Directions:

Question 1:

      a.

      b.

      c.

      d.

      e.

Question 2:

      a.

      b.

      c.

      d.

      e.

Question 3:

      a.

      b.

      c.

      d.

      e.

Question 4:

      a.

      b.

      c.

      d.

      e.

Question 5:

    a.

    b.

    c.

    d.

    e.

Question 6:

    a.

    b.

    c.

    d.

    e.

Question 7:

    a.

    b.

    c.

    d.

    e.

Question 8:

    a.

    b.

    c.

    d.

    e.

Question 9:

    a.

    b.

    c.

    d.

    e.

Thank you for your candid responses.

Data Collection Tool 3.21. MULTIPLE-CHOICE FORM (continued)

Frame 3.10

Ethics Checklist

Did I . . .

	Yes	No	Doesn't Apply
let my institution know about my research plans?			
let my institution know the purpose of my study?			
follow my institution's policies and guidelines in my plan?			
consider my institution's calendar and activities?			
protect the identity of my institution when necessary?			
let parents know the purpose of my study without using jargon or technical language and in their own language?			
let guardians know that their child does not have to participate, without using jargon or technical language and in their own language?			
let guardians know that their child won't be punished for not participating, without using jargon or technical language and in their own language?			
let guardians know of any rewards or benefits and/or risks for their child, without using jargon or technical language and in their own language?			
let guardians know, without using jargon or technical language, that their child can withdraw at any time?			
have children assent to their participation using an age-appropriate and home language?			
protect my participants' identity?			
let my participants know, without jargon and in their own language, that I'll do my best to protect their identity and what I'll do if it is compromised?			
tell my participants, without jargon and in their own language, that they do not have to participate?			

Did I . . .

	Yes	No	Doesn't Apply
let participants know, without jargon and in their own language, that they will not be punished for not participating?			
let participants know, without jargon and in their own language, of any rewards or benefits related to the study?			
keep any financial incentives to a minimum, if provided at all?			
do all I could to protect my participants, socially, physically, emotionally, and mentally?			
let participants know, without jargon and in their own language, that they can withdraw at any time?			
tell participants about any risks involved with the study, without jargon and in their own language?			
plan to attend to any cultural considerations related to the participants?			
consider my own cultural biases, perceptions, values, attitudes, and beliefs in planning?			
consider linguistic differences between myself and my participants?			
plan to use culturally responsive actions in my activities?			
ask only absolutely necessary personal information?			
inform my participants or their parents, without using jargon and in their own language, that I will share with them the findings from my study?			

DATA ANALYSIS AND DISPLAY

The fourth phase of an action research project is data analysis and display. In this phase you will sort out the data collected during the implementation phase. You will organize, sort, compare, contrast, and/or categorize the data collected. After the data have been analyzed, your next task is to create displays of your findings in clear and honest ways. Section 4 contains three subsections: sorting frames, displaying frames, and organizing frames.

Frame 4.1, "From Implementation to Analysis," will help you to think about your analysis from a global perspective. On the first lines you will write the purpose of your study. (If you have forgotten the purpose of your study, you can find it in the first section of your report.) After recording your purpose, you will write your research question or questions in the first column, list key activities in the second column, enter the data sources in the third column, and record your initial thoughts about your study in the fourth column.

DATA-SORTING FRAMES

Next, you will find a series of frames-to assist you in sorting out your data. Ten sample sorting frames are provided in this section. You will select one or more of the options presented. Again, the frames should be considered as tools in a toolbox. Just as each home construction or repair task requires the use of selected tools, so does each action research project require the use of selected tools. You should use only the frames that suit you and your study. Before you select the frame or frames you will use to sort your data, think about the kind of data you collected, the collection schedule, and how the data answer your research question.

Frame 4.2, "Pre- and Post- Table," will be helpful if you wish to determine the changes from pretest to post-test. In the first column write students' names. In the second column record the score on the pre-measure. In the third column record the post-measure. In the fourth column differences in the pre- and post-measures can be recorded. Remember that differences can be positive or negative. The fifth column is a place for you to record any thoughts that you have while sorting pre- and post-measures.

At the bottom of the table there is an opportunity to record group averages for pre- and post-measures and the difference in group performance. In the first and second cells of the bottom row you can record group averages for the pre- and post-measures. In the third column, you might want to record the difference in pre- and post-measure averages or you may want to record the number of students who showed an increase in achievement, the number of students who showed no gain or loss, and the number of students who exhibited a decrease in achievement. In the far right cell in the last row you can note any thoughts that were recurring in the fifth column. You might want to use this fifth cell to record any trends you see in the notes.

Frame 4.3, "Criterion Table One," is a sorting table that may be helpful to you if you are interested in comparing how different criteria were and were not met. If you choose to use this, you will enter selected criteria in column one. You will record the number of individuals meeting the criteria in column two and the number of individuals not meeting the criteria in column three. Column four provides a space for you to record any thoughts that you have while sorting. At the bottom of the chart, space is available to record totals. Again, in the last cell you can note any thoughts that were recurring or record any trends you see in the notes.

Frame 4.4 is similar to Frame 4.3. The only difference is that a column has been added to permit recording a partial meeting of criteria. Frame 4.4 can be completed as Frame 4.3 was completed. It also has a similar use.

Frame 4.5, "Checkpoint Table," provides a way to record measures of success at a number of checkpoints. This frame will be useful if you collected data at multiple times. In the first column you will record student names. In columns two through six you can record performance from the first through the fifth data-collection point. Although there are five checkpoint cells, you do not have to have five checkpoints. Use only the number of columns you need in your study. Again, the last row and the last column allows for the entry of totals or averages.

Frame 4.6, "Skills Table," is a frame that can be used to record skills attainment. In the first column you will write students' names. In columns two through six you will record levels of skills attainment. In these columns you can record attainment in a variety of ways. You might use a + to indicate attainment and a − to indicate a lack of attainment. Alternatively, you might enter a number indicating the degree of attainment, such as 4 for full attainment, 3 for nearing attainment, 2 for limited degree of attainment, 1 for not attained, and 0 for did not attempt. These are just two examples of how you might use Frame 4.6. You may be able to think of others more useful for your study. As in the other sorting tables, the final row and column provides a space to record averages or totals. Beneath the table is a rectangle to identify the skills referenced in columns one through six. Record what each skill is in this box to help you keep track of what skills you are documenting.

Although you have been provided a variety of sorting tables in Frames 4.2, 4.3, 4.4, 4.5, and 4.6, you may find you need to create your own sorting table. One way to create this table is to sketch it on paper. Using a pencil

to write initial labels for rows and columns might help you avoid frustration if you need to adjust the form as you develop it. Another way you may elect to create a sorting table is by using features found in a computer program, such as the table function in Microsoft Word or the graphing function in Microsoft Excel.

Frame 4.7, "Theme Sorting," was designed to create spaces for sorting out themes. If you choose to use this frame, you will be able to record three kinds of information: the theme, examples of the theme (data), and the number of times you found examples of the theme. In each small box you will identify the theme you found as you examined the data. In the larger boxes below each small box you will record evidence of the theme. You may also want to note how many times you observed each theme. You can record this information following the "N =" space in the large box.

Frame 4.8 is a Venn diagram for sorting data. This form would be helpful if you are interested in attending to overlapping issues. If this frame seems helpful, you will record categories in the three small boxes surrounding the loops. Inside each loop you will jot keywords representing data collected within the corresponding category boxes. The small box with "N =" inside it can be used to record a count of each section of the diagram. The diagram can be enlarged if that is helpful to you. You can also make a Venn diagram with two loops or a Venn diagram with more than three loops.

Frame 4.9, "Artifacts Sorting Table," will help you consider and organize work samples, photographs, or artifacts. In the first column you will note the work sample, photograph, or other artifact. You might find it helpful to number or code each item in order to make using the frame easier. If you choose to number or code items, simply write the numbers or code marks on the items in the cells of column one. In column two you will write a caption for each item listed in column one. This is important because you have experiences that let you put the items in context. For example, someone not in your setting may see smiling faces in a photograph, but what makes that photograph important is the fact that a child in the photograph is holding up six fingers, which was the correct answer to a math word problem. In column three you will jot down how each item answers your research question. By answering how each item answers the research question, you will be better able to avoid selecting cute items that don't really answer your question.

Frame 4.10 was created to help you select powerful narrative. In this table you will begin by recording narrative passages in column one. Because you are closely connected to the passages and know their context, you will be better able than your readers to interpret just what the passages mean. Perhaps a short story will best demonstrate why you interpret the passages. If you heard Emma say, "Let's go in the den and trade titties," you might be a bit shocked. Let me interpret for you. My preschool grandchild substitutes "t" for "k," so, with my interpretation, you will see that she wants to trade kitties with me. If I further extend the interpretation for you, sharing what I know from the context of the conversation, you will know that the meaning in her comment was more like, "Let's go in the den and trade kitty stickers." After you have recorded powerful passages and have given them clear and honest interpretations, you will record the meanings you give to the passages in column two. In the third column you will note how the passages answer your research question. Again, considering how the passages answer your research question will help you make wise selections.

Frame 4.11, "Transcribing Form—Video or Audio," was designed to give you a place to keep track of the data you are using from video or audio sources. On the line above the table you will write the name of the disc, tape, or file. In column one of the table you will write down the numbers that help you relocate the specific spot in the source that you are studying. In the second column you will place symbols that help you classify the data. For example, you might use a series of dashes (---) to indicate a pause or an exclamation point (!) to indicate emotional tone, such as excitement. In the third column you will record your transcription of the data source. In lieu of this frame, you might first transcribe the data source and then code it with symbols or colors after the transcription is complete. You might also use one of the tables provided in this section to keep a tally on critical events in the audio or video source.

Frame 4.12, "Conversation Analysis," provides a framework to tally features of verbal interactions in group settings. You can use this form in two ways. First, you can complete the preliminary lines prior to a group meeting and use the columns in the table beneath the preliminary lines to keep track of observed verbal interactions. If you use the frame in this way, it can be a data collection tool. If you record interactions, you can use this frame to categorize interactions as you study the recording. In either event, keeping a key to your recordings will make the analysis more meaningful.

Frame 4.13, "Discourse Analysis," is another way to organize and give meaning to conversations. Prior to analyzing the conversation you will complete the preliminary lines and write a conversation sample in the box that follows. After selecting and writing the conversation sample, you will record features of the conversation in the appropriate columns in the table. Again, keeping a key will help you keep track of your shorthand used in columns.

Frame 4.14, "Word Count and Membership Categorization Analysis," is another way to consider group workings. This frame allows you to study how members of the group are interacting. You may use this form to collect data in direct observations or to analyze recorded data. After completing the preliminary lines, you will write group members' names in column one. In column two you will record critical words and in column three tally how often the speakers use the word. In the final column you will write what role the speakers are taking in the interactions. (See Jorgensen & Phillips, 2002; Reis, 1983; Sacks, 1992; Wetherell, Yates, & Taylor, 2001.)

Frame 4.15, "Theory Building Frame," provides a framework for a three-step analysis. In the first table, you will record pieces of data in column one, and in the second column you will categorize the piece of data. In the second step, you will regroup items by subgroups in column one and record the categories they represent in the second column. In the third step, table 3, you will assimilate the categories and subgroups into an emerging theory. (See Straus & Corbin, 1990, for more information on constant comparative method and grounded theory.)

Frame 4.16 is provided as a tool to use with early language learners or children with language development delays or challenges. Early childhood educators and speech pathologists are sometimes interested in studying the average length of children's meaningful speech units, or utterances, over time or in relationship to developmental milestones. Because children may not always speak in complete sentences, utterances are identified as meaningful chunks of speech. Frame 4.16 provides a frame for studying the length of children's speech samples. After completing the preliminary lines of the frame, in which you will write the child's name, the date, and the setting, you will proceed to the first box and record a language sample. After you have recorded the language sample, you will identify and circle meaningful chunks of speech or utterances. Subsequent to circling meaningful chunks of speech you will identify each utterance with a number. A unit number is the number you have assigned to each utterance. For example, the first meaningful chunk of speech will be numbered "1," the second unit will be numbered "2," and so on. Beneath the language sample box and on the left of the page, you will find the second box, where you will write the identifying numbers of the utterances (the unit numbers) in the first column of the box. In the second column you will enter the number of words that the child spoke in each corresponding unit. In the third box, located to the right of the second box and below the language sample box, you will calculate the mean (or average) length of the utterances. On the top line write the total number of utterances. On the second line write the total number of words. On the third line write the answer you get when you divide line two by line one. In the last box on the frame you may keep any notes you need as you study the language sample. For example, you may wish to record gestures or other nonverbal means of communication.

Frame 4.17 helps you do calculations that assist you in identifying the midpoint of scores or measures of central tendencies. The first measure of central tendencies presented is the mean or arithmetic average. The first box of Frame 4.17 is provided to help you calculate an average for an individual or group. Sometimes action researchers are interested in finding the average score for an individual. If you are studying one person's scores, you will need to count the number of scores you have recorded for the individual and record the number of scores on the number of scores line in the first box. Next, you will add all of the scores together and write the sum of all of the individual's scores on the second line. The final step in finding the average is to divide the sum of the scores by the number of scores. You will record the answer on the third line in the box. You have just recorded the average.

Other times action researchers are interested in finding the average scores of a group. If you are studying the average of the averages of individuals in a group, you will need to use the procedures indicated in the first box for each individual and record their averages in a table or a list where you will list the names of the individuals followed by their average scores. When seeking the average for a group, you will work with the collection of averages. You count the number of individual averages you have calculated on the first line of the box. On line two you will write the sum of all the average scores. And on line three you will write the answer you get when you divide the sum of the average scores by the number of scores. In other words, you will write the average or arithmetic mean on the third line.

The second box provides a space to determine the median score or the midpoint of a list of scores. First, you will need to rank every score and list them from the highest to the lowest scores in the box. If a score occurs more than once you will need to record it every time it occurs. For example, your first score may be 100 and then you may have three scores of 98 followed by a score of 94. Your ranked list would include one entry of 100 and three entries of 98 followed by the score of 94. After listing *all* of the scores, you will count halfway up or down the list and circle that score, which is the median score.

The third box provides a place to reveal the score that occurs most often. Again, you will list all of the scores from highest to lowest in the mode box. You will then study the list to find out which score appears most frequently. You will circle that score because it is the mode.

The fourth box on this frame is a place to record the range or span of the scores. The range is not a measure of central tendencies, but it is often used along with a measure of central tendencies. To identify the range you will write the lowest score on the first line and the highest score on the second line. The breadth of scores from the lowest to the highest score is the range.

In Frame 4.18 a series of questions are provided to help you consider the data you have sorted in the frames you used to begin your analysis. This frame, "Questions for Analyzing," provides twenty-one questions to consider as you sort out and organize your data. The questions were created to help you identify patterns, trends, themes, changes, and order. As you use the questions to think about your data, you will record your responses in the spaces provided. Not all of the questions will relate to all kinds of data collected. You will answer only the queries that help you consider how your data answer your research question. These are sample questions, commonly answered by action researchers, but there may be other questions that you will employ.

DISPLAYING DATA

Once your data have been considered, analyzed, and/or sorted out you will need to consider how best to display your analyses or findings. This section includes examples of figures and tables for representing your analysis of the data. In this section, I will discuss using tables, graphs, and diagrams. The discussion will accompany related examples of ways to present your findings with these kinds of graphic representations of your findings.

Tables are one appropriate way to represent a summarization of findings. Table 4.1 is from a study that was designed to learn how many action research projects were taking place related to curriculum topics at three universities over a five-year period. The table summarizes percentages of curriculum projects by year. Although the percentages appear to be presented from highest to lowest, the table was organized by year.

In some instances, such as in Table 4.2, data are arranged by rank. This table is from a study about what students reported learning in a culture course. The table

Table 4.1. Topics Table

Percent of Curriculum Topics

Academic Year	Percent
1999–2000	76%
2000–2001	67%
2001–2002	54%
2002–2003	50%
2003–2004	26%

shows the number of responses ranked from most often mentioned to least often mentioned. It was designed to show this ranking of each of the categories.

Sometimes chronological order and rank orders are not the purpose of a table. Table 4.3 shows how a table can be used to display a list. You can see that there are no numbers in this table. Instead, a selection of teachers' comments about what they learned in a grant project are listed, and my interpretation of their meaning follows the sample.

Table 4.4 demonstrates how a table can be used to make comparisons between groups. This table displays the perceptions from two groups of students about which courses in their programs influenced their topic selection for their action research projects. The courses are listed in alphabetical order.

Although it is possible to construct a table with pencil and paper, the results can look less than professional. Using a computer program to create your tables will improve their appearance. You will find the table option in Microsoft Word, and Excel also provides useful tools in creating tables.

Other models, such as the series of graphs in Figure 4.1 through Figure 4.10, help to display numerical relationships in a pictorial way. If you choose to use a

Table 4.2. Rank Table

Student Comments by Rank

Domain	Number
Understandings and Appreciation	22
Behaviors	14
Self-Awareness	11
Dispositions	10
Knowledge	8
Skills	8
Total Comments	73

Table 4.3. Comments Table

Representative Comments from "Three Most Important Things I Learned"

"Math concepts can be taught in all subjects" (math across the curriculum)
"Students can surprise you with what they can do" (focus on children's strengths)
"Let children experiment and learn" (importance of manipulatives, exploration, story, etc.)
"Students can understand concepts that they can't always verbalize" (math/language connection)
"Young children need time to have experiences before operations are introduced" (age-appropriate expectations)
"Math includes much more than paper and pencil" (understanding nature of mathematics)
"Young children are hungry for math" (child-centered curriculum)
"Children enjoy math. Math can be fun and kids can still learn" (appropriate pedagogy increases learning)
"How to use fair shares to teach fractions and our responsibility to get children ready for formal study of fractions" (assuming responsibility to lay groundwork for higher math)
"Using snack time for math concepts" (use of routine events to teach math)
"Children can use the not concept" (holding high expectations gets high results)

graph to show your findings, you will need to carefully consider which kind of graph will best represent the story your data are trying to tell. If you want to show a trend, your data can be represented by a line graph, such as Figure 4.1. This graph shows the trend for the number of curriculum projects over time represented in Table 4.1, the table showing the number of curriculum projects over a five-year period.

Figure 4.2, a bar graph, compares categories of action research topics selected by groups of students attending three universities. The bars in the graph allow the reader to quickly compare the three groups.

Figure 4.3 is a pictograph, which is similar to a bar graph and serves a similar function. In this kind of graph, symbols or pictures are used to indicate an assigned quantity. Just as in the bar graph, the pictograph allows the reader to quickly compare groups. This pictograph is a sample that is not connected to a study.

Figure 4.4, a pie graph, is used to show part–whole relationships. The data included in Table 4.2 were used to create Figure 4.4. This graph allows the reader to

quickly compare the amount of each category of comments and see their relationship to the total amount.

Again, you may be attempted to make graphs by hand, but a computer program will make more professional-looking graphs. Just as when creating tables, Microsoft Excel and Microsoft Word are useful tools for creating graphs.

Table 4.4. Comparison Table

Comparison of Topic Selection and Course Influences by Students

Course	SV	OU
Advocacy	0	3
All-program	2	2
Curriculum	4	1
Home/school	2	3
Literacy	2	0
Math	2	0
Multiple	4	4
Practicum	2	0
Research	0	2
Technology	3	0
Theory	0	2
Total projects	21	17

As mentioned in previous paragraphs about graphs, the data presented in Table 4.1 and Table 4.2 are the same data that were presented in the graphs in Figure 4.1 and Figure 4.4. This is not an accident. These selections were made purposefully to make a point about using tables and graphs. Sometimes tables are most appropriate ways to present your data, but other times you need to take one more step in the search for the best way to show your data. If you have displayed your findings in a table, take a minute and consider if a table or a graph would be the best way to put forth your findings. You may find that a graph is a good replacement for a table. Obviously, an unranked list is not a logical table

to put in graphic form. On the contrary, data sets that make comparisons are good candidates for graphs.

In addition to numerical relationships displayed in graphs, you may have relationships not quantified. This was the case in a list type of table. Sometimes a graphic representation of data is helpful to your reader, but a graph doesn't always make sense. A variety of diagrams may be created to show different kinds of relationships. Diagrams such as those in Figure 4.5 through Figure 4.10 may be a better fit to your findings than a table or a graph.

One relationship you may need to show is an overlapping relationship. A Venn diagram, such as Figure

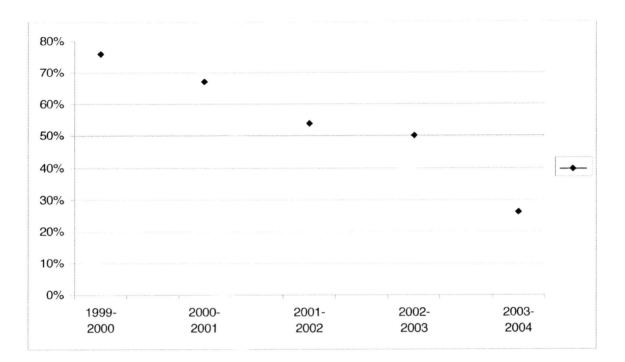

Figure 4.1. Line Graph
Percent of Curriculum Topics by Year

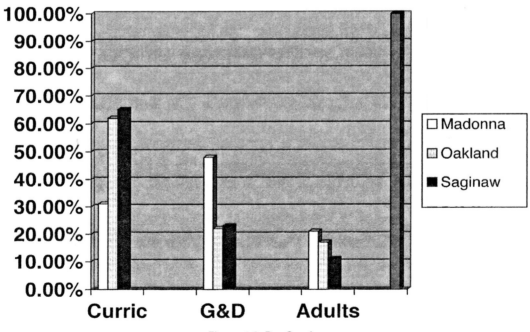

Figure 4.2. Bar Graph
Topic Selection By Topic

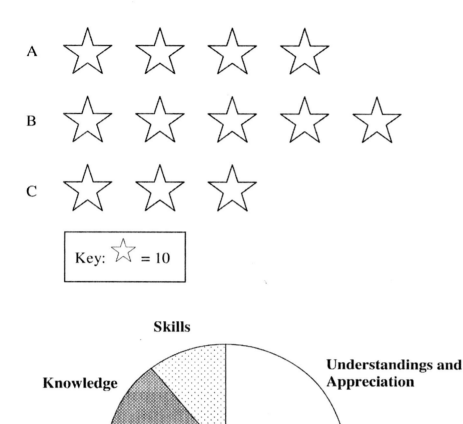

Figure 4.3. Pictograph

Figure 4.4. Pie Graph
Student Comments

4.5, is a useful technique to show relationships with intersections or overlaps. This diagram shows how three categories of research projects overlapped. The intersection of adult support and curriculum shows that some projects involved both adults and curriculum issues. A second intersection is between adults and development. A third intersection is between development and curriculum. In addition, adult support, curriculum, and development each stood alone. In all projects, children were at the center of the projects. This is a unique form of a Venn-type diagram because the center is not the typical intersection of all three areas studied.

Figure 4.6 is an example of a flowchart. Flowcharts are useful to show how things are done, to indicate how things fit together, or to indicate steps in a process. In Figure 4.6 the flowchart shows initial steps in selecting a research topic. It is a type of flowchart that shows a decision-making process.

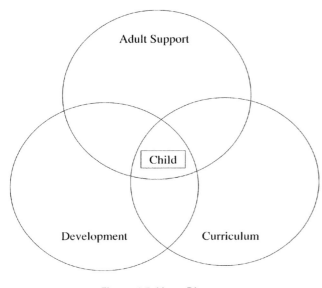

Figure 4.5. Venn Diagram

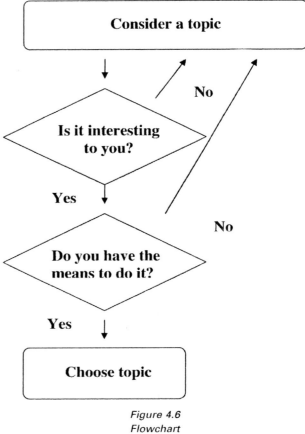

Figure 4.6
Flowchart
Choosing a Research Topic

Figure 4.7 is an example of a diagram of a branching relationship. The diagram shows subgroups in a study about curriculum issues. This diagram resembles a flowchart as it focuses on components of curriculum projects rather than describing a process, indicating steps, or showing how the curriculum issues fit together.

Figure 4.8 is an example of a diagram created to show hierarchical relationships. In this case, it shows the professional sequence in a teaching program. The initial coursework forms the base upon which a practicum rests. The practicum experience provides the base for an action research project, which in this program is the capstone experience.

Figure 4.9 provides a frame to show how multiple findings relate to one other. In this figure, the interactive relationships between infants and family members and the one-way interaction of media influence are displayed. The arrows show the direction of influences.

A figure such as Figure 4.10 is useful to illustrate nested relationships. In this diagram, a child lives within a family and the family functions within a society. In this case, the larger unit, society, contains each of the smaller elements.

In this second section of the chapter, "Displaying Data," you have been presented with fourteen tables and figures that each represent a unique way to show your data. As you carefully consider your data and the story they want to tell, you will need to think about and select the figures and tables that best tell your data's story. You want to use tables and figures to make your presentation of data as clear as you can.

In addition to models for representation, which tend to provide the big ideas or summaries of the findings, action researchers often include critical incidents—important work samples, relevant stories or journal entries, vital quotes, essential photographs, or other such important events or artifacts—throughout the text of the fourth narrative section of the research study. Using these kinds of data will give depth to your displays. You may use these kinds of displays alone or in conjunction with one or more of the fourteen types of tables and

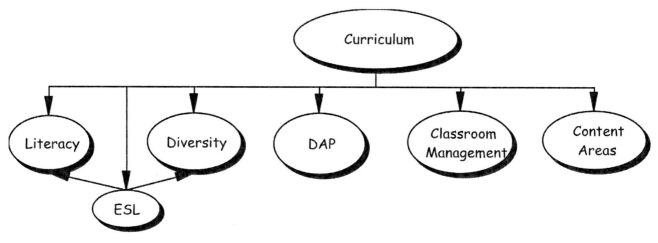

Figure 4.7. Organizational Chart

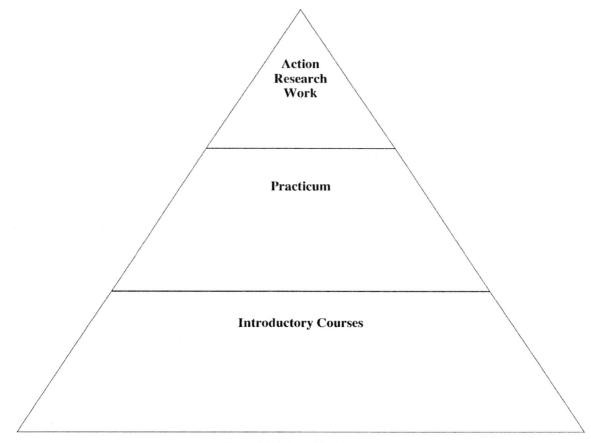

Figure 4.8. Hierarchical Diagram
Education Program

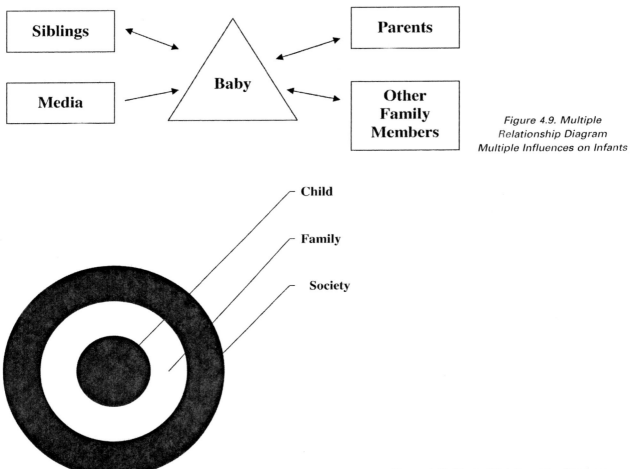

Figure 4.9. Multiple Relationship Diagram Multiple Influences on Infants

Figure 4.10. Nested Relationships Diagram

figures presented in the "Displaying Data" section of this chapter. You may also be doing a study in which a model is not appropriate. You may have a series of critical incidents that don't require the use of a model. Again, the goal is to allow the data to tell their story.

ORGANIZING FRAMES

Following the analysis frames comes Frame 4.19, "Organizing the Analysis," which will help you organize your tables and figures for presentation. This frame was designed to help you prepare for writing about the analyses of various data. In the first column you will record the research question(s). It need not be written in each cell of the first column, but recording it just prior to writing helps to keep it fresh in your mind. In the second column

you will bullet key findings from your analyses of the data sources. You did your analysis in Frame 4.1 through Frame 4.18 in the "Sorting Frames" section of this chapter. In the third column you will record the related figure for each key finding. After you decide which artifacts (worksamples, quotes, photos, etc.) will accompany your tables and figures, you are ready to write the fourth part of your action research report.

Finally, Frame 4.20, "Analysis and Display—Ethics Checklist," provides a framework to make sure you have used ethical methods of analyzing your data and selected appropriate models for displaying your analyses. Use this checklist to review your work and make sure you are presenting a professional and principled analysis of the data report.

From Implementation to Analysis

Purpose of Study: _____

_____

Research Question(s)	Actions to Answer Question(s)	Documentation Collected	Preliminary Impressions

Frame 4.2

Pre- and Post- Table

Student	Pre-	Post-	Change	Notes
Average				

Criterion Table One

Criteria	Yes	No	Notes
Totals			

Criterion Table Two

Criteria	Yes	No	Partially	Notes
Totals				

Checkpoint Table

Student	Check-point 1	Check-point 2	Check-point 3	Check-point 4	Check-point 5	Total or Average
Average/Totals						

Skills Table

Student	Skill 1	Skill 2	Skill 3	Skill 4	Skill 5	Skill 6
Totals/Average						

Skill 1=	Skill 2=	Skill 3=	Skill 4=
Skill 5 =	Skill 6=		

Theme Sorting

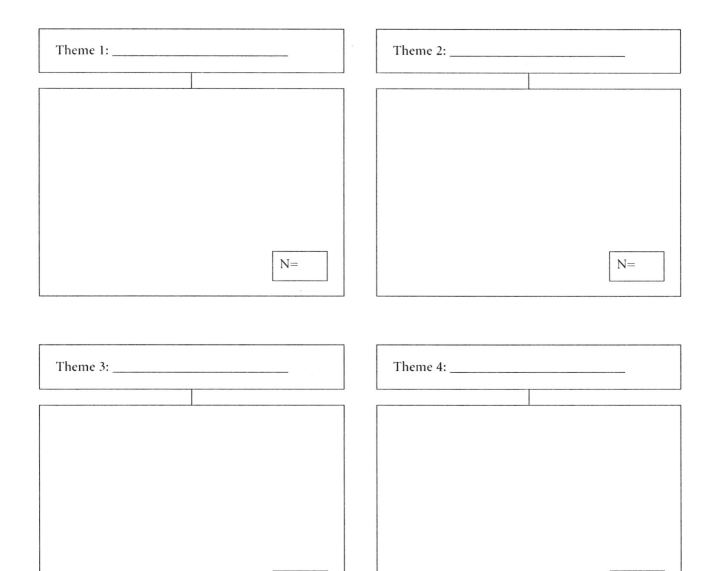

Theme 1: _____

N=

Theme 2: _____

N=

Theme 3: _____

N=

Theme 4: _____

N=

Frame 4.8

Venn Diagram

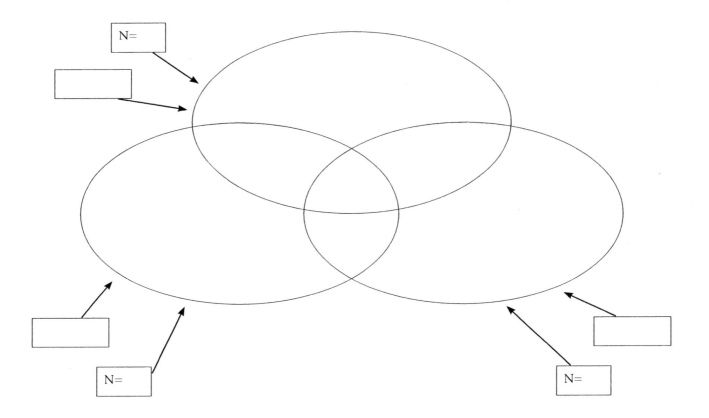

Artifacts Sorting Table

Sample (Worksample, photo, illustration . . .)	Caption	How does it help answer the research question?
1.		
2.		
3.		
4.		
5.		
6.		
7.		
8.		
9.		
10.		
11.		
12.		
13.		
14.		
15.		
16.		
17.		
18.		
19.		

Selecting Powerful Narrative

Samples	Meaning	How It Answers the Research Question

Transcribing Form—Video or Audio

Tape or disc identification: _____

Location information	Symbol	Transcription

Conversation Analysis

Group: _____ Date: _____

Setting:_____

_____

Turn taking	Accounts	Formulations	Preliminaries	Adjacent pairs

Key

Discourse Analysis

Group: _____   Date: _____

Setting:_____

_____

Conversation Sample

How is language used to make sure language is significant?	What activities are occurring?	What identities is this language used to enact?	What kind of relationship does the language seek?	What social goods does this language perspective hold?	What connections does this language build?

Key

Word Count and Membership Categorization Analysis

Group: _____ Date: _____

Setting:_____

_____

Name	Word	Use Tally	Membership Group

Membership Group Key

Theory-Building Frame

Step 1: Initial Sorting

Meaningful Piece of Data	Emerging Category

Step 2: Creating Subgroups

Subgroup	Categories

Step 3: Assimilation of Sorting

Emerging theory

Frame 4.15 THEORY-BUILDING FRAME (continued)

Mean Length of Utterance Analysis Sheet

Name: _____ Date: _____

Setting:_____

_____

Language Sample

Unit Numbers	Number of Words

Total number of utterances: _____

Total number of words: _____

Average length of utterances: _____

Notes:

Frame 4.17

Measures of Central Tendencies Calculations Sheet

Calculating Mean Score

The number of scores is _____.

When I add all the scores together I get _____ for the sum.

When I divide the sum by the number of scores the answer I get is _____.

Calculating Median Score

List scores from high to low. Circle the middle score.

Calculating Mode Score

List scores from high to low. Circle the score that appears most often.

Questions for Analyzing

1. What events seem to be recurring? List them and tally them below.

Event	Tally

2. What kinds of gains are made or lost over time?

Observed Event	January	February	March	April	May

3. How do the pre- and post-measures compare?

Student	Pre-measure	Post-measure

4. What kinds of errors were made in the beginning? How have they increased or decreased over time?

Type of Error	September	October	November	December

5. What is the average of the responses? (What are the most frequently occurring responses?)

Response	Time 1	Time 2	Time 3	Average
Average				

6. What is the average of the scores?

Scores by Student	Time 1	Time 2	Time 3	Average
Average				

7. What patterns are there in the interactions?

8. What is the average rating of _____?

9. What happened least often to most often? How did items rank?

10. What ratios are there between _____ and _____?

11. In what sequence do events occur?

12. What kinds of differences are there between _____ and _____?

13. How are _____ and _____alike?

14. What meanings are given to key words or phrases?

15. How did initial behaviors change over time?

Frame 4.18 QUESTIONS FOR ANALYZING (continued)

16. What preferences became evident?

17. What common events occurred across or within populations?

18. What themes were frequently evident?

19. What patterns appear again and again?

20. What patterns are unique?

21. What steps did participants use during the implementation phase?

Frame 4.18 QUESTIONS FOR ANALYZING (continued)

Organizing the Analysis

Research Question(s)	Key Findings	Displays

Analysis and Display—Ethics Checklist

Did I . . .	Yes	No	Doesn't Apply
collect enough data to honestly answer my question?			
interpret data in a culturally appropriate manner?			
avoid cultural biases as I studied the data?			
report my findings in a clear and appropriate way?			
do my best to protect my participants' identity?			
do my best to keep my own biases in check as I analyzed the data?			
avoid omitting data that told a story I didn't like?			
use data responsibly?			
keep my promises to my participants and institutions as I analyzed the data?			
choose models that honestly represent my work?			

DISCUSSION, IMPLICATIONS, CONCLUSIONS

The fifth and final phase of the action research project brings you full circle in your study. In section 5 you will discuss the findings from your study as they relate to your research question and how your findings relate to the findings of others who have studied your topic. You will discuss how your professional views have changed or sharpened. You will draw conclusions from the findings and make recommendations for your future practice. After you are sure that your work in chapter 5 meets professional ethical standards, you will edit your work and put all five sections of your report together.

Section 5 has three frames and five figures. The frames were created to help you compose chapter 5, and the five figures were included to serve as possible models for your preliminary pages. Therefore, you will complete Frame 5.1 through Frame 5.3 and consider Figure 5.1 through Figure 5.5 as ways to put the finishing touches on your project report.

Frame 5.1, "Planning the Discussion, Implications, and Conclusions," is designed to help you consider key components in the discussion of your findings. As you complete this first frame in section 5, you should think about your research question and the purpose of your study. As you record your research question and purpose in the first box, consider how your findings relate to your question and your purpose for doing the study. By taking time to consider and write the research question and purpose of your study, you are refocusing yourself on what you hoped to learn from your work.

Having recorded your research question and purpose for the study and having refocused on what you hoped

to learn from the study, you are now ready to answer the question(s) you posed in the first section of your project. In order to answer your question(s) you will need to revisit section 4 of your report. Think about how the data you presented in section 4 answers your research question(s). Now, record in the second box how the data that you generated and presented in section 4 of your report answer your research question and meet the purpose of your study.

Just as you returned to the first section of your report to reconsider your research question(s) and then revisited the fourth section of your report to connect your findings to your research question prior to completing the second box of Frame 5.1, you will now return to your review of the literature to complete the third box in Frame 5.1. You will reread your review of the related literature and think about how what you found in your study compares to what the authors you cited in the review of the literature found. You can examine how your findings may agree with, disagree with, or partially agree with the findings of the authors you cited. As you think about this, write your findings, the cited authors' findings, and the cited authors' last names in the third box of Frame 5.1.

Once you have listed how the key findings answer your research question and how they compare with the critical work in your review of the literature, you will continue your reflection. Now you will contemplate how your thinking has changed as a result of conducting your study. In the fourth recording box of Frame 5.1 you will list how your views have changed, solidified, or expanded as a result of the findings of the study.

Based on the reflections that you recorded in the first through fourth boxes of Frame 5.1, you will record in the fifth recording box implications for your practice. In other words, you will list what your findings and reflections imply for future professional practice.

In the sixth and final box of Frame 5.1, you will draw conclusions about your work and record them. You will list key points that will bring the discussion and the project report to a close. Having completed the "Planning the Discussion, Implications, and Conclusions" frame, you are ready to write the fifth section of your report.

Once you have written a draft of section 4 of your report, you will use Frame 5.2. This frame is an ethics checklist. Just as in the previous sections, it is important to present your work in a professional and principled manner. Completing the ethics checklist for section 5 will help ensure that you do present your work in an ethical way.

Frame 5.3 is a checklist to help you put the project together in a professional, satisfying format. This final frame is a checklist designed to assist you in editing your study report. After your report is edited, beginning with the first section and ending with the fifth section, you are ready to compile your report.

You may wish to add a report cover, a title page, a dedication page, an acknowledgments page, and a table of contents page. Samples of these pages follow in Figure 5.1 through Figure 5.5. These examples are only samples. You may have unique requirements for formatting these preliminary pages. If that is the case, you will follow those directions for completing the preliminary pages.

After the whole report is completed and bound, I ask my students to consider two final matters. First, think about how you can share what you have learned as a result of your study. Second, take time to savor your accomplishment. You have completed important work. Congratulations!

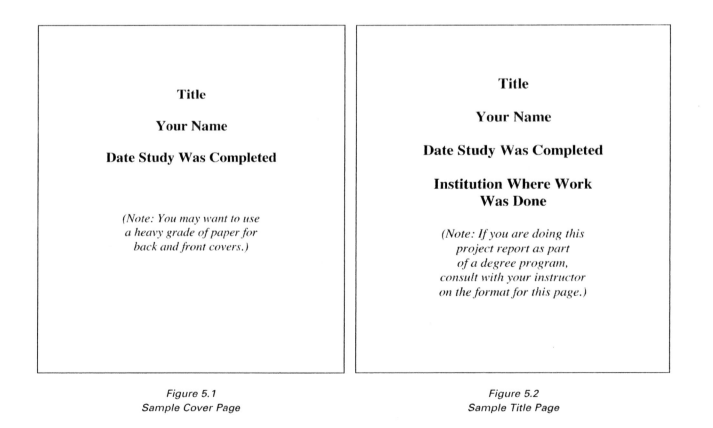

Title

Your Name

Date Study Was Completed

(Note: You may want to use a heavy grade of paper for back and front covers.)

Figure 5.1
Sample Cover Page

Title

Your Name

Date Study Was Completed

Institution Where Work Was Done

(Note: If you are doing this project report as part of a degree program, consult with your instructor on the format for this page.)

Figure 5.2
Sample Title Page

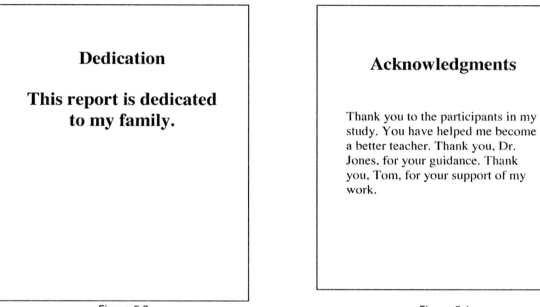

Dedication

**This report is dedicated
to my family.**

Figure 5.3
Sample Dedication Page

Acknowledgments

Thank you to the participants in my study. You have helped me become a better teacher. Thank you, Dr. Jones, for your guidance. Thank you, Tom, for your support of my work.

Figure 5.4
Sample Acknowledgments page

Table of Contents

Figure 5.5
Sample Table of Contents Page

Planning the Discussion, Implications, and Conclusions

Revisit the research question(s) and purpose of the study.

Write your research question here.

Write the purpose of your study here.

Key points in discussion of how the findings answer your research question(s).

1.

2.

3

4.

5.

Key points in discussion of how the findings relate to the literature discussed in the review of the literature (identify the point and the author).

My Findings	Author's Findings	Author's Name
1.		
2.		
3.		
4.		
5.		

Key points in discussion of how your views have changed, solidified, or expanded as a result of the study.

1.

2.

3.

4.

5.

Frame 5.1 PLANNING THE DISCUSSION, IMPLICATIONS, AND CONCLUSIONS (continued)

Key points in discussion of the implications of your study.

1.

2.

3.

4.

5.

Key points for conclusions.

1.

2.

3.

4.

5.

Frame 5.1 PLANNING THE DISCUSSION, IMPLICATIONS, AND CONCLUSIONS (continued)

Frame 5.2

Discussion, Implications, and Conclusions—Ethics Checklist

Did I . . .	Yes	No	Doesn't Apply
base all of my findings in data?			
avoid cultural biases as I discussed the findings?			
avoid cultural biases as I discussed implications?			
avoid cultural biases as I discussed conclusions?			
fully cite comparison studies?			

Frame 5.3

Final Editing Checklist

Check to see if . . .	Yes	No	Notes on changes
subjects and verbs agree			
tense remains consistent			
nouns and pronouns are consistent (singular—singular or plural—plural)			
pronouns have the antecedent nouns			
pronouns and antecedent nouns agree			
pronouns are correctly placed			
misplaced or dangling modifiers are avoided			
sentences do not end with prepositions			
adjectives and adverbs are correctly placed			
I have avoided sentence fragments			
I have avoided run-on sentences			
apostrophes are used correctly			
commas are used to separate			
commas are used to set off			

Check to see if . . .	Yes	No	Notes on changes
colons and semicolons have been used correctly			
parentheses and brackets have been used correctly			
periods are in place and extra periods have not been left during the cutting and pasting of text			
exclamation points are minimal or are not used at all			
hyphens have been used correctly			
capitalization is used correctly			
abbreviations and acronyms are spelled out initially in the text			
I have avoided wordiness			
direct quotes are in quotation marks and fully cited			
all tables, figures, and charts are correctly labeled			
all work samples and photographs have appropriate captions			
all numbers are written out when they less than 10			
all sources are listed in alphabetical order on the reference page			
all citations are complete			

Frame 5.3 FINAL EDITING CHECKLIST (continued)

Did I . . .	Yes	No	Notes on changes
complete a spelling check?			
complete a grammar check?			
save changes in the grammar and spelling checks?			
make sure I checked for spelling that spell check might have missed (e.g., too, to, two)?			
avoid ending sentences with etc. and so on?			
protect the identity of study participants consistently?			
check to make sure page numbers in the table of contents are correct?			
make sure appendices are correctly labeled?			
make sure appendices are in correct order?			
make sure I followed the style manual instructions?			
make clear and helpful transitions between paragraphs?			
make sure the document flows from section to section?			
make sure the document flows from beginning to end?			
make sure I can be proud of the final product?			

Frame 5.3 FINAL EDITING CHECKLIST (continued)

References

Alber, S. M., Edgerton, S., & Kypros, B. (2006). Longitudinal study: Effects of action research on educators' professional growth. In A. Salhi (Ed.), *Excellence in teaching and learning: Bridging the gaps in theory, practice, and policy* (pp. 57–68). Lanham, MD: Rowman & Littlefield.

Altrichter, H., Posch, P., & Somekh, B. (1993). *Teachers investigate their work: An introduction to the methods of action research.* London: Routledge.

American Educational Research Association. (2002). *Ethical standards of American Educational Research Association.* Washington, DC: Author.

American Psychological Association. (2003). Guidelines on multicultural education, training, research, practice, and organizational change for psychologists. *American Psychologist, 58* (5), 377–402.

American Psychological Association. (2009). *Publication Manual of the American Psychological Association* (6th ed.). Washington, DC: Author.

Apps, J. W. (1988). *Higher education in a learning society: Meeting new demands for education and training.* San Francisco: Jossey-Bass.

Apps, J. W. (1992). *Adult education: The way to lifelong learning.* Bloomington, IN: Phi Delta Kappa Educational Foundation.

Calkins, L. M. (1994). *The art of teaching writing.* Portsmouth, NH: Heinemann.

Calkins, L. M., Hartman, A., & White, Z. (2005). *One to one: The art of conferring with young writers.* Portsmouth, NH: Heinemann.

Calkins, L. M., & Harwayne, S. (1987). *The writing workshop: A world of difference; A guide for staff development.* Portsmouth, NH: Heinemann.

Clay, M. (2000). *Running records: For classroom teachers.* Portsmouth, NH: Heinemann.

Duckworth, P. A. (1973). *Construction of questionnaires. Technical study.* ED 138 610.

Hollins, E. R. (2006). Transforming urban schools. *Educational Leadership, 63* (6), 48–52.

Johnson, D. W., & Johnson, R. T. (1990). *Learning together and alone: Cooperative, competitive, and individualistic learning.* Boston: Allyn and Bacon.

Johnson, D. W., Johnson, R. T., & Holubec, E. J. (1993). *Cooperation in the classroom.* Edina, MN: Interaction Books.

Jorgensen, M., & Phillips, L. (2002). *Discourse analysis as theory and method.* Thousand Oaks, CA: Sage.

Kinchole, J. (2003). *Teachers as researchers: Qualitative inquiry as a path to empowerment.* London: Routledge/ Falmer.

Knowles, M. S. (1980). *The modern practice of adult education: From pedagogy to andragogy.* Chicago: Follett.

Knowles, M. S. (1990). *The adult learner: A neglected species.* Houston: Gulf Publishing.

Miles, M. B., & Huberman, A. M. (1994). *Qualitative data analysis: An expanded sourcebook.* Thousand Oaks, CA: Sage.

Miller, D., & Pine, G. (1990). Advancing professional inquiry for educational improvement through action research. *Journal of Staff Development, 11* (3), 56–61.

Mills, G. (2003). *Action research: A guide for the teacher researcher* (2nd ed.). Upper Saddle River, NJ: Merrill.

Paivio, A. (1990). *Mental representations: A dual coding approach.* New York: Oxford University Press.

Reis, H. T. (1983). *Naturalistic approaches to study social interactions.* San Francisco: Jossey-Bass.

Sacks, H. (1992). *Lectures on conversation.* Cambridge, MA: Blackwell.

Silverman, D. (2001). *Interpreting qualitative data: Methods for analysing, talk, text and interaction.* Thousand Oaks, CA: Sage.

Straus, A. L., & Corbin, J. M. (1990). *Basics of qualitative research: Grounded theory procedures and techniques.* Newbury Park, CA: Sage.

Tomal, D. R. (2003). *Action research for educators.* Lanham, MD: Rowman & Littlefield.

Wetherell, M., Yates, S., & Taylor, S. (2001). *Discourse theory and practice: A reader.* Thousand Oaks, CA: Sage.

About the Author

Sandra M. Alber is associate professor of education at Oakland University. She has mentored hundreds of action researchers since 1992.